The Utopian Flight from Unhappiness

The Utopian Flight
Freud against Marx

from Unhappiness:

on Social Progress

Martin G. Kalin

Nelson-Hall nh Chicago

ISBN 0-911012-65-6

Library of Congress Catalog Card No. 73-80500

Contents

II
The Antiutopian Critique

Introduction

George Wald once remarked that a typical American university might refuse to hire Darwin on the grounds that his comprehensive knowledge could not be condensed and packaged as a respectable academic specialty. Professor Wald's own Nobel Prize in biochemistry indicates that he has impeccable credentials as a specialist; hence his appraisal of contemporary higher education adds to his judgment the weight of authority. But perhaps Wald is wrong in this respect: even if the sciences should reject Darwin's application, surely the humanities would accept it without hesitation. Such optimism rests on the mistaken supposition that the humanities remain a haven in which the perennial issues of life, those apparently insoluble problems of general concern, can be discussed with impunity and even encouragement. A glance at scholarly journals in literature, philosophy, and similar fields should acquaint the naïve with the facts of academic life.

Unfortunately, however, no convenient demon stands behind Darwin's fictional misfortune. The fault does not lie simply with the trend toward specialization, which has gained such momentum since the 17th century; the obvious benefits of science and technology would be impossible apart from this trend. Further, the scientists themselves offer few legitimate scapegoats; major figures such as Einstein and Wald show a profound grasp of life beyond their disciplines. Finally, the blame cannot be laid on the already stooped shoulders of the humanities; under the influence of benign neglect they have been forced to ape the specialization in the sciences in their pursuit of the usually elusive government grant. Since no obvious culprit seems available the best protest of the Darwin affair may be simply a discussion of one often ignored issue.

Among the many questions that have been raised, none rivals the deceptive simplicity of: What makes man unhappy? Proposed answers appear innocently abstract until one recalls that Marx's cry for revolution echoed his analysis of man's unhappy condition; thus a theory about unhappiness may have extraordinary practical ramifications. The aim of this book is to investigate two conflicting kinds of answer, christened *utopian* and *antiutopian*; they just as easily could have been called the *optimistic* and *pessimistic* answers. The choice of Marx and Freud to speak for the utopian and antiutopian positions, respectively, stems from two considerations. First, each figure inaugurated a revolution in theory that has had profound consequences in the practical order. Second, the depth and rigor of each thinker's system supply the incentive for further reflection on the problem of unhappiness.

The distance between the utopian and antiutopian positions can be charted roughly as follows. The utopian analysis of unhappiness expresses hope for the future by its adherence to two principles. The first states that man has enough pliability to allow transformation of his presently unhappy condition into a happy one; or, in more prosaic terms, the race is not doomed by an immutable nature to remain unhappy. The second principle asserts that a sufficient change in the environment (both physical and social) can accomplish a corresponding alteration in the human condition, or, simply stated, an improvement in man's surroundings can make him happy. The second principle need not reflect a simple-minded belief that man merely reacts to fortuitous changes in his circumstances. Marx, for instance, emphasizes that man himself plays the key role in altering the environment; thus man transforms himself by transforming his surroundings.

The antiutopian rejoinder centers on a denial of the first principle (transformation) in favor of the dictum that a permanent core in man's nature condemns him to unhappiness. Although the antiutopian position acknowledges that the human condition can be improved, perhaps by restructuring the environment, it stops short of equating such improvement with even the near-elimination of unhappiness. Thus the antiutopian forecast is that man must continue to endure unhappiness as part of his inalterable fate.

A more precise clarification of the differences between the utopian and antiutopian positions must await the chapters on Marx and Freud, but a cautionary note about these chapters is in order here. The discussion uses Freud's theory about the instincts to criticize Marx's utopian vision; however, the discussion proceeds on the assumption that Marx's views deserve serious attention despite their failure to withstand an antiutopian critique.

Two special procedures have been adopted for examining and evaluating the writings of Marx and Freud. First, every technical term is clarified in ordinary English, thereby opening the discussion to anyone with the interest and patience to explore difficult issues. Second, most of the disputes that surround the interpretation of texts are confined to the notes—a practice that must be adopted if the discussion is to highlight the issues rather than the immense amount of commentary that has grown around the works of the two thinkers. However, any radical departure from a standard interpretation of Marx or Freud is justified in the body of the discussion.

Finally, the ambitions of a study like this one should be stated at the outset. Clearly the problem of unhappiness cannot be solved even at a theoretical level in these pages; indeed the problem remains available for discussion precisely because of its resistance to solution. Thus no final answer to the question about man's unhappiness will be attempted here. The forthcoming look at a utopian and an antiutopian response to the question can be justified, however, with a slogan to which both Marx and Freud subscribe: No problem can be solved rationally until it has been understood.

I
The
Utopian
Dogma

The hovels of the real world continue to exist despite the speculative palace built by the philosopher.

Kierkegaard

I
The End of Illusion as a Prelude to Happiness

The Theory and Practice of Revolution

Marx enjoys an enviable position among Western intellectuals because his ideas have had such a clear impact on history; hence he cannot be treated as just another star in a constellation of luminous minds. Since the association of Marx's name with major political and social movements tends to distract attention from his contributions as a theoretician, an evaluation of his thought requires that distinctions be drawn among: (1) his own theory of history; (2) closely associated theories, such as Leninism; (3) purely ideological or polemical uses of his doctrines; and (4) nontheoretical activity that derives its inspiration ultimately from (1). The present work will concentrate on (1) with emphasis on its relationship to (3) and (4); little consideration will be given to (2). The following terminology should prove helpful in keeping original Marxism separated from its various offspring. The term *Marxian* is reserved for (1); the adjective *Marxist* applies to both (1) and (2). Thus Lenin's teaching about the concentration of power in an elite Communist

3

Party qualifies as Marxist but not Marxian. Finally, the noun *Marxism* will designate Marx's own *theoretical* work.

Marxism can be characterized roughly as a theory of revolution in the service of revolutionary practice, and Marxian theory promotes revolution by debunking the illusions that help to deter it. Marx therefore directs his message ultimately at the proletariat on the conviction that the truth will send it down the revolutionary road to freedom. The exact way that Marxism contributes to revolution will be discussed in Chapters 2 and 3; the task here consists in outlining the connection between the theory and the practice of revolution.

Theory as an Aid to Revolutionary Practice

A clarification of the connection between theory and revolutionary practice should begin with at least provisional definitions of both notions. Theory will be defined tentatively as any systematic explanation. The term *systematic* implies that a theory uses a single conceptual framework to account for seemingly unrelated phenomena. Marxian theory thus qualifies as systematic because it uses the same set of categories in explaining such apparently diverse matters as economics and religion; that is, it explicates both of these phenomena with such notions as class, alienation, and labor. To describe a theory as an explanation in no way suggests that it must be true; even a bizarrely false explanation counts as a theory as long as it remains systematic. A comparable definition for revolutionary practice poses greater difficulties because such practice covers all the activities through which a dominated class tries to improve its lot—activities that achieve complete success if the class establishes its own dominance over society. Sometimes a seizure of power by a previously suppressed class may lead to fundamental changes in society. Defenders of the Bolshevik Revolution often insist that it transformed Russia by eliminating oligarchy. It should be noted, however, that revolutionary action may have merely political consequences. In the same illustration, critics of the Russian Revolution may argue that it involved nothing more than an exchange of power between the czars and the Bolsheviks. If revolutionary practice comprises all the activities in which a dominated class engages for the purpose of improving its situation, then such practice also may include theoretical work. Perhaps Marx himself provides the best instance of a theoretician's functioning as a revolutionary. Yet, that theory constitutes only one type of revolutionary practice does not diminish the importance of the distinction between them; no explanation of the unique responsibility Marxism assumes for the proletarian revolution can be given apart from this distinction.

The way theory relates to other kinds of revolutionary practice can be clarified by delineating Marx's position on the proletariat. This class comprises the impoverished and oppressed urban workers, who were especially conspicuous at the outset of the industrial age. Because they lacked wealth, the proletarians naturally lacked the education and other requirements for advancement that the dominant class (the bourgeoisie) possessed. Poverty not only enslaved the proletariat by putting it at the mercy of those whose wealth gave them control over the entire social system; poverty also had the effect of making the proletariat as a whole oblivious to both the real causes of its situation and the proper means of rectifying that situation. This double consequence of poverty becomes clear in light of the notorious conditions that prevailed in industrial societies during Marx's own lifetime (1818-83). After a worker had spent 14 hours at grueling manual labor he had little time and energy for reflecting on the complex factors that forced him to lead such a life; and since in the system children and adolescents entered the ranks of labor they were deprived of the formal education that might have equipped them with the discipline and skill to analyze their problems and fashion remedies. Further, the dominant class generally controls education, entertainment, news, and other forms of communication; hence the media usually promote the interests of the rulers rather than those of its rivals.

Marx characterizes this state of affairs with the remark that the ideas of the ruling class normally constitute the ruling ideas.[1] An example from his work might be welcome here. Adam Smith, proponent of laissez-faire economics, maintains that man has an innate propensity to "exchange and barter," and under capitalism this inclination manifests itself as economic competition among individuals.[2] Once such an idea becomes well entrenched people assume that society must be built on a foundation of competitive economics, for a noncompetitive system seems to frustrate one of man's "natural drives." Marx charges that Smith's views on man protect capitalism because they automatically discredit any program of revolution. If these views win wide acceptance within the proletariat they will tend to make the class docile by fostering among its members the conviction that society *should* be economically competitive, even if such competition condemns most proletarians to stay at the base of the social pyramid. In summary, Marx believes that ruling class ideas indoctrinate the proletariat to accept its station under capitalism.

Marx's belief that the proletariat lacks an adequate understanding of both its problem and the right solution can be expressed in more general terms; namely, the class remains largely unaware of its mission to destroy capitalism. Marxian theory predicts the eventual replacement of capitalist by communist society, and it regards the proletariat as a key force behind the anticipated transition. But Marx recognizes that the proletarians cannot be expected to undertake a revolution until they have become convinced that it alone can improve their condition, for this conviction must offset two psychological factors that discourage revolutionary action: the fear of punishment or even death, and the hope for reform within the system. If more than luck is to determine the success of their mission the proletarians also must understand the established order well enough to know how it can be destroyed. For one, the proletarians must appreciate that capitalism can be eliminated only if they seize power from the bourgeoisie, who, in turn, will seek to maintain a system that favors them. These and related prerequisites for the proletariat's deliberate destruction of capitalism can be abbreviated by saying that the class must become enlightened before it can accomplish its mission.

The manner in which Marxism functions as revolutionary practice now can be stated with greater precision; namely, it enlightens those who otherwise might remain oblivious to their mission as revolutionaries. The various kinds of enlightenment Marxism provides cannot be enumerated here; selected examples must suffice. According to Marx, capitalism constitutes just one phase in the evolution of society; hence the unnecessary prolongation of the system impedes the natural course of man's development. In affirming the intrinsically transitory character of capitalism Marx counters the suggestion of a bourgeois intellectual like Smith that the system uniquely accords with human nature. Further, Marx's analysis of capitalism links its economy with the exploitation and degradation of its citizens, especially the proletarians; thus he indicts capitalism on the basis that it pays for an economic miracle with misery. Finally, Marx describes certain developments within capitalism that should lead to its downfall; the creation of the proletariat under this system is a case in point.

The preceding discussion indicates the sense in which Marxian theory qualifies as revolutionary practice. The theory seeks to equip the proletarians with the knowledge or consciousness necessary for fulfillment of their mission by enlightening them in such matters as the justification and rewards of a revolt against the bourgeoisie. Thus Marxism aims at transforming the proletariat—the impoverished and almost powerless victims of capitalism—into a viable political force that will annihilate the system. That transformation takes place when members of the class become aware of the real causes of their condition and the appropriate remedies.

Enlightenment of the proletariat, though, cannot be understood merely as education of the ignorant, because illusion rather than a simple lack of knowledge prevents a proletarian revolution. Marx therefore approaches the task of enlightenment with the conviction that the proletarians *profoundly misunderstand* their condition. Instead of recognizing themselves as members of a class whose destiny consists in overthrowing capitalism, they believe in the permanence of the system; and the belief takes on the appearance of a self-fulfilling prophesy to the extent that it discredits even the idea of moving beyond capitalism. Moreover, the proletariat binds itself to a bourgeois code of morality that condemns the kind of violence usually attendant in revolution. The proletariat inhabits a world of illusions that drain its potential for revolution; consequently it cannot perform its mission until its consciousness has been cured. Marxism attempts to provide a cure by debunking or demystifying the false suppositions that almost ensure that the proletariat will take no drastic action against capitalism.

These topics are treated more fully in later chapters. Meanwhile it will be useful to consider one way that Marxian theory seems to subvert revolutionary practice.

Theory as a Deterrent to Revolutionary Practice

Different factors militate against the translation into practice of Marx's doctrine about revolution. His reliance on a technical vocabulary as well as his often ponderous style compound the problem of transmitting very difficult ideas to the uneducated; hence Marxism has found its most hospitable reception among intellectuals rather than among proletarians. (Lenin, Trotsky, Rosa Luxemburg, and Mao amply illustrate the point.) This point deserves attention here because it suggests that Marxian theory cannot have its intended effect without the aid of the intelligentsia, although such aid may take various forms. Intellectuals, for instance, may confine their efforts to education on the belief that the proletariat can make its own revolution once it has understood enough about Marxian theory; or they may reject this approach in favor of building an elite, which then directs the revolution by a still unenlightened proletariat. Lenin's break with orthodox Marxism occurs at just this juncture; namely, he advocates establishment of a vanguard—the Communist Party—which masterminds the proletarian revolution *before* educating the other revolutionaries.

In any case, intellectuals who take on the responsibility of helping to implement Marx's theory of revolution face "the dilemma of conscience."[3] Marxism is allegedly a science. Its author places his own work among masterpieces in natural science. In an allusion to Newtonian mechanics, for example, Marx characterizes his theory of history as a study of the "laws of motion" operating in society.[4] He also approves the suggestion that Marxism extends the theory of evolution. Just as Darwin specifies the laws of biological development, so Marx reportedly discloses the laws that govern social change and progress.[5] The scientific stature of Marxism will not be disputed for the moment; the important matter here concerns the intellectuals' response to its predictions about the demise of capitalism.

To say that Marxian theory enjoys the status of a science implies, among other things, that solid evidence stands behind its forecasts; otherwise its promise of a communist utopia deserves the same condemnation and ridicule that Marx reserves for wishful thinking and romanticism of any sort. But if the transition from capitalist to communist society cannot be prevented, then the question arises why anyone (especially an intellectual) would risk his own position by taking an active part in an apparently inevitable turn of events. The question has been answered in different ways. It has been proposed that the desire to swim with rather than against the tide of history can induce a disciple of Marxism to play even a dangerous role in the proletarian revolution; sometimes opportunism alone may supply the incentive. A more sophisticated response[6] is that Marxism does not pretend to guarantee the inevitability of the movement from capitalism to communism; instead, the theory indicates the likely direction of social evolution. Thus, Marx's forecast about the advent of communism must be read as a well-founded projection rather than a rash prophesy; he promises the appearance of a communist system only on condition that the laws previously and presently governing history continue to do so. This interpretation thus weakens Marx's claims about the future so that they become hypothetical statements: *if* the proletariat becomes aware of its mission, and *if* this class seizes power from the bourgeoisie, and *if* . . . , then communism will replace capitalism.

The addition of such qualifications to his predictions protects Marx from the embarrassment of having a straightforward prophesy falsified, but it also intensifies the "dilemma of conscience," which now can be stated with accuracy. The dilemma arises because a convert to Marxism must decide whether to complement his belief in the theory with the appropriate action. Thus an intellectual who agrees with Marx that the proletariat should overthrow capitalism faces the decision of translating his conviction into practice by, say, making the proletariat aware of its mission. Conscience enters the dilemma because the convert's options have a moral dimension. His refusal to promote revolution, for example, appears morally reprehensible in light of his commitment to the righteousness of the proletariat's cause.

The connection between the intensity of the dilemma and the "weak" interpretation of Marx's predictions requires clarification. Marx's forecast about the movement from capitalism to communism can be interpreted as a (1) nonhypothetical or (2) hypothetical claim. If a convert to Marxism subscribes to (1), then his decision about participating in the proletarian revolution lacks moral urgency. He can watch from the sidelines as the "inevitable" victory of the proletariat unfolds, or he can join the struggle. His choice seems relatively unimportant because, in his own mind at least, the revolution's success does not depend on his contributing to it.

If the convert adheres to (2), however, the moral overtones of his decision become pronounced. The second reading implies that each person can help to ensure the transition to communism by fulfilling a condition stated in an *if*-clause of Marx's prediction.

As a previous example indicates, an intellectual can promote the communist utopia by educating the proletariat about its mission, for, according to (2), this utopia will become reality *if* the proletariat understands its mission, and *if* this class seizes power from the bourgeoisie, and so forth. Thus acceptance of (2) places a very heavy burden of responsibility on every Marxist, because this reading suggests that even one person's refusal or failure to act on behalf of the revolution may prevent society from completing its evolutionary course at communism. In slightly different terms, the second interpretation of Marx's prediction makes the appearance of a communist system contingent on an indefinitely large number of individual decisions; each decision therefore becomes crucial for the realization of his forecast.

This digression into possible interpretations of Marx's prediction has not singled out his own stand on the matter. Although his writings never deal explicitly with the issue, Marx indicates his position in other ways. His tone in stating his forecast reveals his conviction that capitalism *necessarily* will give way to communism; and that he adds no qualifications to this prediction certainly suggests a strictly nonhypothetical reading of it on his part.[7] In summary, Marx evidently subscribes to the "thesis of inevitability." The suggestion here has been that this thesis might dissuade a convert to Marxism from risking his own welfare by entering the proletarian struggle, which initiates the movement from capitalist to communist society; for if the victory of the proletariat seems assured from the outset, then only the voice of conscience—or the worst type of opportunism—presumably could impel a rational person to take part in a venture that might cost him his life. Finally, if the thesis deterred enough Marxists from either promoting the revolution or participating in it, then the transition to communism would be placed in jeopardy.

Marx shows little interest in this line of reasoning. His work concentrates on analyzing the forces that advance society toward the goal of communism, and since Marx himself belongs to the capitalist era he highlights its place in social evolution. Obviously the forces in question include a human element; the proletarians, for instance, must take power from the bourgeoisie in order to set the stage for the appearance of communism. Marxism, though, does not consider man's role in social change to the extent that it studies the dilemma of conscience. The point at present is not that Marx should be faulted for not paying sufficient attention to this specific topic. Nonetheless, his apparent disinterest in the dilemma provides an indication of what may be the most serious flaw in his theory—its inadequate and unconvincing analysis of man.

Marxism and Its Intellectual Background

This chapter has sketched the lines of inquiry to be pursued in the discussion of Marxism. Despite added detail, the dominant themes will remain the same: how Marxian theory aids the practice of revolution by penetrating the illusions that impede it; how this theory suffers from an unsatisfactory account of man. The first step toward clarification of these topics consists in setting Marxism against the background of its intellectual ancestors, particularly traditional Western philosophy. The contrast should permit a better explanation of how Marx's own theoretical work promotes the revolution he predicts.

2
Marx and the Unkept Promises of Western Thought

Marxism and Polemics

The often impassioned polemics that surround Marxism have been guided by at least one shared assumption. Both those who hail Marx as a secular messiah and those who damn him as a Machiavellian demon agree that his message centers on the theme of revolution. Obviously this agreement has not diminished the mutual hostility of the disputants; instead, it has become another basis for charge and countercharge. Thus Marxists condemn as reactionary any action that impedes revolution, while anti-Marxists insist that revolutionary upheavals usually cause more misery than they cure. Further, these disputes often reveal only the insincerity or ignorance of their participants. Proponents of Marxism may seize its doctrine of revolution in trying to sanctify crass political expediency, as in the Stalinist era when terrorism was justified as a necessary safeguard for the victory over the czars. On the other side of the ideological barrier, condemnation of Marxism may be more visceral than rational, as when American politicans exploit an uncritical equation of Marxism with opposition in general. These abuses of Marxism do more than just reflect certain unhappy facts about current affairs; they distract attention from a theory of history that deserves serious consideration. Accordingly, this chapter will avoid polemics so that Marx's views on revolution can be judged on their own merit.

Throughout the discussion Marx's theory of revolution will be located within the tradition of Western thought. This procedure can be justified initially because Marx was above all a theoretician of revolution despite his promotion of and participation in political activity. The point can be further clarified by contrasting Marx with some of his famous followers. The writings of a Marxist such as Stalin (and to a lesser extent Lenin and Mao) warrant attention principally because of their author's political achievements. But Marx's accomplishments as an activist hardly rival his contributions as a theoretician, and his reputation as a noteworthy thinker would be intact even if his ideas had not become associated with successful revolutions. In brief, Marx was an intellectual. Failure to qualify this characterization would distort his position, for Marxism represents an ingenious attempt to narrow the gap between the theory and the practice of revolution without obliterating that distinction. The remainder of this chapter will trace Marx's efforts to integrate his own revolution at a theoretical level into other kinds of revolutionary action.

Marx and Traditional Western Philosophy

Marx couches his theory of revolution in notoriously difficult language. Key terms such as *class* and *capital* have imprecise and even inconsistent meanings. Marx also incorporates the jargon of various disciplines into his writings; in *Capital*, for example, he enriches the vocabulary of economics with expressions from philosophy. Although Marx cannot be excused for the resultant obscurity one thing must be said in his defense. The success of his project demands certain liberties in his use of language; specifically, words must move freely across the traditional boundaries that separate disciplines. Thus a word such as *class* ordinarily occurs in such fields as sociology and political theory; in Marxism, however, this word also belongs among the central terms of economics and history. More accurately, Marx repudiates traditionally fixed disciplines and seeks to replace them with a new theoretical enterprise, which he names "the materialist conception of history."[1] Instead of relying heavily on neologisms in stressing the novelty of his "new materialism," Marx uses the terminology of established disciplines in an unprecedented manner. As a result some confusion in his presentation of his own ideas seems unavoidable.

The present concern with Marx's use of words stems from the idea that shifts in his terminology indicate changes in his thought. The general movement in Marxian theory can be charted in this way. The early Marx comes across as an indignant humanist who abhors the discrepancy between the ideals of Western civilization and social reality. His criticisms have a sarcastic and righteous tone; his language abounds with such philosophical terms as *alienation*. The later Marx tries to assume a more objective or scientific stance. He often drops his earlier vocabulary in favor of jargon from economics, and his writings seem more sober despite their critical content.

The transition from the early to the mature Marx has been an item for intense scholarly debate[2] that sometimes has assumed strong polemical and political overtones. For example, interest among Eastern bloc intellectuals in the early or more philosophical writings often represents a rebellion against official, doctrinaire, and sterile brands of Marxist thought; conversely, the concern among Western thinkers with these same works frequently comes from a desire to make the chief theoretician of communism palatable for capitalist consumption. Details of this debate cannot be given here. It suffices to note that scholars on both sides of the question acknowledge a development in Marx's ideas; their primary disagreement is whether this development should be described as evolutionary or revolutionary. As a first step in defending the thesis that a continuity in the content of Marxism outweighs variations in its presentation, let us examine the philosophical tradition from which Marx broke.

As a young philosopher completing his doctoral dissertation Marx appeared to be entering a field that already seemed fully cultivated. Hegel's thought so thoroughly satisfied the current appetite that the need for further nourishment appeared unlikely. But Hegel's reputation did not rest exclusively on a talent for originality; evidently he had written the eulogy for Western philosophy by so successfully fulfilling its ambitions, which, with their Hegelian fulfillment, can be characterized roughly as follows. First, Western philosophy has attempted to be *systematic* by furnishing one framework for all knowledge, and Hegelianism brings such diverse fields as logic and history under a single system. Second, Western philosophy has tried to be *comprehensive* by encompassing every area of experience, and Hegelianism covers the data of history, ethics, anthropology, mathematics, natural science, social theory, economics, psychology, logic, art, religion, and previous philosophy. Third, Western philosophy has sought to be *scientific* by enumerating the laws that phenomena obey, and Hegelianism specifies the laws that govern reality. Fourth, Western philosophy has aspired to be *metaphysical* by disclosing the basic nature of things, and Hegelianism reduces all reality to consciousness.

Naturally these four points might be expressed in a different fashion, and with enough ingenuity they could be condensed into a single formula. They also gloss over important differences among philosophies because of their generality. Nevertheless, the list can provide two services in the present discussion. First, Marx's disenchantment with Western philosophy can be clarified with reference to it. Second, a common misconception about Marx's break with Hegelianism in particular can be explained in terms of the four points.

Marx felt that the project of Western philosophy ended with Hegelianism, since this system had accomplished each of the tasks that comprised the project. Thus Hegelianism could not be faulted as an inadequate or unfinished philosophy, and a critique of it implied an attack on philosophy itself—hence Marx's insistence that the proper criticism of Hegel involves going beyond philosophy. The manner in which Marx proposes to transcend philosophical thought in general and the Hegelian example in particular has been a source of confusion for which Marx himself bears partial responsibility. Sometimes he suggests leaving philosophy in favor of revolutionary action. "The philosophers have only *interpreted* the world in various ways; the point, however, is to *change* it."[3] By injecting a little zeal into his works Marx occasionally promotes the false impression that he intends to forsake thought for action. Yet even after his break with philosophy Marx does not give up a theoretical stance toward reality; he remains an intellectual. Marx's critique of philosophy centers on the contention that the discipline does not offer even a *theoretically* adequate interpretation of reality; therefore philosophy cannot aid the revolutionary transformation of society. Once the rupture with philosophy has been accomplished, Marx undertakes the task of constructing a new discipline (namely, his "materialist conception of history"), which can function as a suitable replacement. The suitability of this new theory will depend on its ability to serve the needs of the proletarian revolution.

In summary, Marx's case against philosophy does not rest on the trivial objection that philosophy as a form of contemplation (theory) differs from revolution as a form of noncomtemplative action (praxis).[4] On the contrary, he acknowledges that an important and irreducible distinction holds between such theorectical activities as doing philosophy and such practical activities as making revolution. The Marxian critique of philosophy comprises two allegations: first, some types of theory serve the practice of revolution; second, philosophical contemplation does not perform this service.

This discussion has portrayed Marx's break with philosophy in very broad strokes. Important details to be added include: indication of a common misconception about Marx's disavowal of Hegelianism; analysis of ways in which Hegel and Marx differ on a specific issue; and, finally, examination of Marx's alternative to philosophy.

Hegel and Marx on Metaphysics

Some scholars[5] have suggested that Marx's primary disagreement with Hegelianism concerns its particular metaphysical commitment. According to this view (which will be called the "metaphysical reading" of Marx), Marx rejects the Hegelian thesis that reality ultimately reduces to something spiritual or mental; then he presents his own metaphysics in which physical or material reality counts as ultimate. But this interpretation of the Hegel-Marx debate attributes a significant concession to Marx. The point can be clarified with reference to the four ambitions of Western philosophy listed earlier. To characterize Marxism as an intentional metaphysics is to suggest that Marx and Hegel concur that theoretical knowledge should be systematic, comprehensive, scientific, *and* metaphysical. Further, if Marx's chief objection against Hegelianism concerns its specific brand of metaphysics, then he evidently concedes its systematic, comprehensive, and scientific character, for, again, Marx regards this philosophical system as the fulfillment of the ambitions behind Western philosophy.

The metaphysical reading of Marx seriously misrepresents his attitude toward theoretical knowledge; it also overlooks that Marx explicitly rejects at least one metaphysical materialism as an alternative to Hegel's metaphysical idealism. Marx believes that a theory cannot be either *comprehensive* or *scientific* so long as it remains metaphysical. Accordingly, he tries to avoid metaphysics so that he can fulfill two of the other ambitions in Western philosophy: the ambition to cover the major areas of experience and the ambition to specify the laws that govern experience. The question about whether he succeeds in avoiding metaphysical commitments must be postponed; at present the main point concerns his deliberately antimetaphysical approach. The first step toward an antimetaphysical reading of Marxism is to consider the different ways in which Hegel and Marx regard work.

Hegel's main analysis of work occurs in his *Phenomenology of Spirit*, the most familiar statement of his philosophy. The scholarly attention accorded this book has not prevented misunderstandings of its purpose, although the fault lies not so much with Hegel's tortuous prose as with his commentators' failure to analyze the entire *Phenomenology* as one expression of Hegelian metaphysics. The difficulty can be explained by considering the most common misconceptions.

According to one interpretation Hegel seems to present in the *Phenomenology* a chronicle of man's intellectual development; specifically he appears to trace the evolution of civilization by indicating the principal ideas of each epoch. For example, Hegel views the Roman Empire under Marcus Aurelius through its intellectual reflection, the philosophy of stoicism. This reading of Hegel has led some scholars to characterize the *Phenomenology* as "the systematic study of those phenomena collectively describable as the manifestations of the human spirit," or as an "itinerary of the human spirit," which depicts the "cultural adventures of the human species."[6] In short, the *Phenomenology* has been interpreted as a history of man's dominant ideas.

If the above interpretation of Hegel were entirely misguided, its refutation would be an easy matter. But this anthropological reading of Hegel, like the metaphysical reading of Marx, has an initial plausibility that disguises its inadequacy. Although Hegel draws liberally from the data of intellectual history throughout the *Phenomenology*, his avowed purpose in that book is to furnish a metaphysics; he therefore tries to penetrate the facts about cultural development so that he can disclose their metaphysical essence.

Hegel's intention becomes clear in light of his own clarifications of the book's title. As a "phenomenology" the work represents a systematic study of the manifestations—the phenomena—of spirit or consciousness. But the word *spirit* (Geist) does not designate human consciousness; instead, it refers to what Hegel calls "absolute spirit." A precise understanding of this phrase is not needed here. It is sufficient to note that the descriptive term *absolute* includes among its antonyms the adjectives *human*, *finite*, *limited*, and *imperfect*. Consequently, commentators who read the *Phenomenology of Spirit* as a clandestine piece of theology in which the notion of an absolute spirit replaces the traditional concept of God have at least one advantage over proponents of the anthropological interpretation; namely, the first recognize that the real subject matter of the *Phenomenology* is the evolution of *nonhuman* spirit or consciousness. Thus the *Phenomenology* can be read as a record of man's intellectual history only by ignoring Hegel's warning to the contrary.

Hegel's intention to present a metaphysics in the *Phenomenology* dictates the perspective from which his analysis of work must be viewed. The analysis occurs mainly in the section, "Dependence and Independence of Self-consciousness: Mastery and Slavery." A tentative explanation of the title is that Hegel employs the historical phenomenon of mastery and slavery in order to explicate the notion of self-consciousness as it pertains to absolute spirit; hence he takes an example from human history in clarifying the nature of absolute or nonhuman consciousness. His discussion of the master-slave relation deserves consideration in its own right, and many imitations have flattered it.[7] A rough summary of the discussion and its bearing on the topic of work is sufficient here.

In the philosophical tradition to which Hegel belongs, man stands above the rest of nature because of his unique capacity for self-awareness. Leibniz, for instance, attributes consciousness to every object, including a presumably inanimate thing like a stone, but he ascribes "apperception" or self-consciousness to man alone among created beings. Although Hegel has no quarrel with this characterization of man, he insists that self-consciousness (particularly in the case of absolute spirit) constitutes a *process* through which the self *becomes* aware of itself. In using the master-slave relation to illustrate the point, Hegel evidently draws from the ancient world in which a slave well may be a defeated warrior. The phenomenon of two soldiers engaged in potentially mortal combat emphasizes the unique ability of a self-conscious being to act deliberately, for, at least in Hegel's example, the two combatants enter battle as proof of their courage. Thus the two warriors choose the possibility of even death through combat in order to demonstrate before an equal (namely, the opponent) their ability to act self-consciously. Further, the transformation of two initially brave rivals into a master and his slave (the warrior who disgraces himself by capitulating in the face of death) lends emphasis to the idea that self-consciousness is a process rather than something static. Each combatant gains a new awareness of himself as the one becomes victor and the other his vassal.

The connection between Hegel's example of the master-slave relation and his analysis of work now can be explored. As a vanquished warrior in bondage to his conqueror the slave lives in humiliation, and as a forced laborer he exercises little control over his products. But such labor emancipates the slave in at least one sense. Although work itself does not free him by eliminating his master, it still alleviates his condition. The skills the slave acquires by working equip him to cancel his dependence on the generosity of both nature and other men if he regains his freedom.[8] Work also introduces a permanent quality into his existence. It must be recalled that Hegel regards self-consciousness as the distinctively human trait in man. Consciousness, however, seems to defy description because of its evanescent character. Since consciousness consists of ever-changing perceptions, ideas, feelings, and so forth, consciousness cannot be equated with any particular one of its contents.[9] Nonetheless, consciousness is more than an elusive rhapsody of disconnected mental contents and events, for all of these constantly changing contents and events belong to a single consciousness (for instance, the slave's consciousness). Thus consciousness appears as "pure flux" in light of its transitory contents and events; it also displays structure and constancy because it unifies those fleeting contents and events into a single consciousness. The mysterious nature of consciousness accounts for the metaphoric cast that surrounds descriptions of it. An extreme example, Sartre calls consciousness a "decompression of being" and a "nothingness" that possesses only a "semblance of being."[10]

The way work contributes to the slave's understanding of himself must be brought into sharper focus. The slave cannot get a satisfactory insight into his nature as self-consciousness simply by introspecting, which discloses only the evanescence of consciousness, its apparent lack of an enduring core that can be identified as *the* self. As a worker, however, the slave recognizes himself in his creations. His products, as material or physical *things*, have a substantial quality that his consciousness, as an immaterial or mental *process*, lacks. Thus the slave's products provide a relatively stable and definite expression of himself, and by seeing himself in his product the slave complements the introspective picture of himself as an endless series of ephemeral perceptions, thoughts, and feelings.

Before turning to Marx's adaptation of the master-slave relation, it may be instructive to mention another misconception about the difference between the two thinkers. Marx sometimes receives undue credit for three insights into work. First, work is a social enterprise; it involves the relationship between man and his fellow men just as much as the one between man and the rest of nature. Second, work and social conflict appear inseparable. Third, man transforms himself through work.

Hegel's analysis of the master-slave relation contains a clear statement of each point. He emphasizes that the slave works precisely because the master forces him to. This emphasis indicates Hegel's denial of an instinct to work; he regards social compulsion as a prerequisite for labor. Hegel's statement of the second point seems evident. His main analysis of work occurs within the discussion of mastery and slavery, and, as noted above, he makes work a *consequence* of conflict. Finally, Hegel acknowledges that the slave transforms himself through his work by gaining both skills and an enhanced self-awareness. The primary difference between the Hegelian and Marxian analyses of labor does not stem from a disagreement about some specific aspect or result of this activity; instead, the two accounts diverge because the notion of work assumes different roles in each thinker's system. Stated somewhat differently, Marx and Hegel agree on the principal features of work, but they disagree on the importance that should be assigned to it.[11] The concept of work carries a far heavier explanatory role in Marxism than it does in Hegelianism.

Hegel's analysis of work centers on the way work alters and enhances self-consciousness. The analysis falls largely within the discussion of mastery and slavery, which, in turn, serves as one of Hegel's illustrations for the evolution of absolute spirit. Thus Hegel studies work primarily in order to explicate the central idea of his metaphysics—absolute consciousness. Of course, that he looks at the phenomenon of work in such a light need not invalidate his conclusions about it, but his view shows that the notion of work does not belong among the main categories of his philosophy.

In sharp contrast to Hegel, Marx gives the concept of work a key position in his system. The point becomes clear with respect to Marx's theory of man. As a student of Western philosophy he knew the traditional descriptions of man as a social being, a rational animal, a creature in the image of God, but he emphasizes work in his own definition of man.

> Men can be distinguished from animals by consciousness, by religion, or anything else you like. They themselves begin

> to distinguish themselves from animals as soon as they begin to produce their means of subsistence, a step which is conditioned by their physical organization. By producing their means of subsistence, men are indirectly producing their actual material life. The way in which men produce their means of subsistence depends in the first place on the nature of the actual means of subsistence which they find in existence and have to reproduce. This mode of production should not be regarded simply as the reproduction of the physical existence of individuals. It is already a definite form of activity of these individuals, a definite way of expressing their life, a definite mode of life on their part. As individuals express their life, so they are. What they are, therefore, coincides with their production, both with what they produce and with how they produce.[12]

Although this passage will be fully discussed in Chapter 3, one point deserves immediate attention. If men begin to distinguish themselves from members of other species precisely through their work, then a concrete or empirically reliable theory of man must emphasize—not merely cover—this aspect of human reality. In addition, if the exact manner in which men together produce their "means of subsistence" determines their nature to a great extent, then the various aspects of work must be incorporated into a comprehensive theory of man. The joint requirements of concreteness and comprehensiveness help to explain Marx's dissatisfaction with metaphysics, notably Hegelianism, and his growing interest in such disciplines as economics. These requirements and their influence on the development of Marxism can be clarified further with reference to the master-slave relation.

A superficial comparison of the Hegelian and Marxian treatments of mastery and slavery is this. Marx transforms Hegel's master and slave into capitalist and worker (proletarian), respectively. Like the master, the capitalist enjoys a parasitic existence because he consumes the products of manual labor without having to do any of it himself. The proletarian resembles the slave because he toils under the threat of death. As the member of a propertyless class the proletarian depends exclusively on his wage for survival; hence the capitalist who controls that wage automatically has the power of life over the proletarian. Finally, the material success of capitalism undermines it in much the same way that the master's victory reduces a once-noble warrior to a parasite who could not survive without his slave. Just as the slave's work helps to cancel his dependence, so the proletariat's labor prepares it for liberation.

This reading of Marx cannot be dismissed on the grounds that it misses the mark altogether. Marx exploits the emotional overtones in the equation between the master-slave and the capitalist-proletarian relationship, but the conspicuous debt Marx's critique of capitalism owes to Hegel's analysis of mastery and slavery cannot be allowed to obscure a fundamental difference in their approaches. According to Marx, the antagonism between the capitalist and the proletarian represents the last phase in a prolonged and varied conflict between masters and slaves, and he regards work as the key factor throughout the history of this conflict. Specifically, the division of human beings into oppressors and oppressed reflects different relationships to work. Thus the slave class normally comprises those who own and control little besides their own ability to work. Since such people depend on someone else for the tools or materials to convert their raw potential for work into products, they fall toward the bottom of the social ladder; above them, of course, are those who own and control the "means of production." The point can be abbreviated as the dictum that the phenomenon of work underlies that of mastery and slavery.

Additional details in Marx's analysis of work come later. Note, however, that his analysis goes much further than its Hegelian counterpart. Marx, for instance, studies the laws that govern the production and distribution of commodities; hence his analysis of work includes many contributions from economics. Since work constitutes a social enterprise that generates conflict, he also views it from a sociological and a political perspective. But Marx turns to history as the best treatise on work. History documents the way in which man transforms the entire natural order, including himself, through his labor.

An example may be helpful. The transition from feudalism to capitalism has been attended by a corresponding alteration in man. Several obvious differences between the two cultures provide one measure of this alteration. For instance, a shift in the concentration of population from rural to urban areas has so quickened the pace of life that anxieties that would have been abnormal during the Middle Ages now seem quite respectable. Comparable examples include a change in typical occupations and a rise in the average standard of living. On a more profound level, contemporary industrial societies at least espouse the ideal of democracy; the ordinary citizen of these nations therefore has a picture of himself different from, say, that of a serf in the rigidly stratified feudal society. The step from feudal to industrial man involved many factors; we will consider two of them. First, increased efficiency in agriculture during the Middle Ages freed part of the population from the land, thereby adding a new source of labor for emerging industries. Second, medieval artisans refined their techniques so that production on a mass scale became a real possibility. In cruder terms, the labor of the Middle (and previous) Ages brought about changes in man and his civilization, and labor in the industrial age can be expected to have a similar effect. Thus history shows that man increasingly appropriates and civilizes the rest of nature through his work; he also transforms himself in the process. As a record of what labor *can* accomplish, history furnishes the data for projections about what it *will* accomplish; hence Marx's historical outlook includes a vision of a communist utopia.

This sketch of Marxism has touched on several points where it breaks with Hegelianism on work. The Marxian analysis solicits contributions from various disciplines, excluding metaphysics, but its Hegelian counterpart places the phenomenon of work squarely within the province of metaphysics. Marx regards mastery and slavery as a historical situation that varies according to different relations toward work; so his investigation of the master-slave relation occurs within a more general study—the history of labor. Hegel examines labor as one facet of the master-slave relation, and he studies this relation primarily in order to illustrate the metaphysical notion of self-consciousness. Since the difference in approaches stems from their attitudes toward metaphysics, a discussion of Marx's disenchantment with all metaphysical explanation is necessary.

Metaphysics as Monistic Explanation

Marx raises two distinct but easily conflated objections against Hegelianism. First, he criticizes its idealistic as against materialistic commitment. Second, he condemns its metaphysical as against scientific perspective. These criticisms will be taken in order.

Hegel's metaphysics follows a tradition in Western philosophy by presenting a thesis about the single underlying principle of reality. The thesis, stated roughly, is: the progressive manifestations of the absolute spirit in the process of gaining absolute (namely, perfect or unlimited) knowledge of itself constitutes the whole of past, present, and future reality. In less recondite language, this thesis challenges the classification of entities into the ultimate categories of physical and mental (spiritual). Hegel rejects such a bifurcation on grounds that it holds only for the appearance, rather than the underlying essence, of reality. For instance, a tree usually would be classified as a physical object. According to Hegelian metaphysics, however, every object reduces without remainder to an object *of* absolute consciousness; hence even a presumably material or physical object qualifies as a mental or spiritual entity. Additional acquaintance with the intricacies of Hegel's metaphysics will not be needed in order to appreciate Marx's first objection to it; namely, Hegelianism promotes the worst kind of mystification by denying the irreducibility of material reality. For one, the Hegelian reduction of the material universe to a mere manifestation of the absolute spirit allegedly subverts progress. Marx accuses the idealists in general and Hegel in particular of a propensity for political conservatism because they relegate such ideals as freedom to the realm of thought alone instead of making them part of man's full existence. In brief, the idealists reportedly falsify material life by transforming it into a merely spiritual drama. This objection will be considered again with reference to Marx's discussion of ideology; meanwhile it will be instructive to consider his second objection against Hegelianism.

Failure to distinguish sharply between Marx's two criticisms of Hegelianism leads directly to the metaphysical reading of his works (see "Hegel and Marx on Metaphysics"). This reading draws exegetic support from passages such as: "It is not the consciousness of men that determines their existence but, on the contrary, their social existence determines their consciousness."[13] Such statements imply that Marxism results from a simple inversion of Hegelian metaphysics; namely, Marx reverses Hegel's reduction of matter to (absolute) spirit by making (human) consciousness a mere reflection of man's material existence. Additional evidence for the metaphysical interpretation of Marx comes from his infrastructure-superstructure distinction. He maintains that the economic structure of society constitutes the ". . . real foundation on which rise legal and political superstructures and to which correspond definite forms of social consciousness."[14] In summary, the metaphysical reading of Marx rests on the supposition that he rejects the idealistic slant in Hegelianism without disavowing its metaphysical perspective.

Perhaps the main difficulty with the metaphysical reading of Marx concerns his attitude toward Feuerbach, whom he calls "the true conqueror of the old philosophy" (namely, Hegelianism).[15] Especially in his early works Marx borrows both terminology and substantive tenets from Feuerbach. His acceptance of most of Feuerbach's "transformational criticism" or "inversion" of Hegelian metaphysics can be characterized in the following way. Hegel completely distorts the connection between man as an independently existing particular and one of man's attributes, consciousness. Specifically, Hegel transforms human consciousness into absolute spirit, and he concludes the idealistic distortion of reality by reducing man and every other material thing to an attribute (manifestation, appearance) of absolute consciousness. Feuerbach's inversion restores the commonsensical state of affairs in two moves: first, it discredits absolute spirit as a figment of Hegel's imagination; second, it acknowledges man as independent particular. Thus Feuerbach unmasks the grand illusion of Hegelian idealism, and his own materialism, which makes matter into the ultimate principle of reality, fills the metaphysical vacuum his critique creates. The chief difference between Hegelianism and its Feuerbachian inversion now can be summarized: in response to the Hegelian reduction of nature (matter) to consciousness (spirit), Feuerbach affirms the primacy of matter over consciousness.

Throughout his writings Marx retains a sympathetic attitude toward Feuerbach's effort to raze Hegel's palace of ideas. It would be a mistake, though, to interpret his sympathy as unqualified approval of materialistic metaphysics, for Marx also offers some criticism of Feuerbach's alternative to Hegelianism. He objects to Feuerbach's inversion because it does not escape the domination of *metaphysics*, although it represents liberation from *idealism*. Marx makes this point by asserting that "German criticism" (by which he means the movement of Feuerbach and others away from Hegelianism) still pays clandestine homage to Hegel by adopting his metaphysical perspective. Feuerbach's answer to Hegel does not consist in rejecting metaphysics as such but, rather, in presenting an alternative metaphysical system. Marx states the criticism in this way.

> German criticism has, right up to its latest efforts, never quitted the realm of philosophy. Far from examining its

general philosophical premises, the whole body of its
inquiries has actually sprung from the soil of a definite
philosophical system, that of Hegel. Not only in their answers
but also in their questions there was a mystification.[16]

According to Marx, Feuerbach's failure to throw off the
Hegelian commitment to metaphysics has dire consequences. Feuerbach's preoccupation with finding a substitute for absolute spirit
as the foundation of reality detracts from his assessment of even
the material universe. First, simplism infects the Feuerbachian doctrine that nature (matter) constitutes the metaphysical basis of reality.
By "nature" Feuerbach means a static system of material objects,
including man; he therefore ignores the way work continuously
transforms nature. Stated somewhat differently, Feuerbach's
materialism makes little provision for the dynamic interaction
between man and the rest of the material world; and whenever
he manages to account for such interaction he reportedly falls back
on idealistic explanations.[17]

In discrediting metaphysical materialism Marx singles out a
theory of causality for which he often receives the blame. The theory
states that the material universe relates to man's consciousness as
cause to effect; hence the theory promotes the simplistic view that
consciousness changes in direct accord with its material circumstances. Marx rejects this position because it ignores the reciprocal
causality between man as a conscious being and his environment.
For instance, although the typical worker under capitalism differs
in temperament and outlook ("consciousness") from his ancestors
in agrarian society, it must be remembered that capitalism is to
some extent man's intentional creation. Thus man sometimes acts
deliberately or consciously to change his material circumstances,
which, in turn, affect his consciousness. Marx therefore rejects any
brand of materialism that recognizes only unilateral causal relations
going from nature to man and his consciousness.

Marx's disenchantment with Feuerbach's philosophy as the

paradigm of metaphysical materialism now can be summarized. Marx rebukes Feuerbach for his failure to appreciate the dynamic character of nature, and Feuerbach stands guilty because he overlooks work's influence on the very constitution of nature. To claim that Feuerbach's materialism does not comprehend man's special role within the natural order is just another way of saying that this materialism does not deal with history, for history can be viewed as the collective process through which man transforms all of nature, including himself. From the Marxian standpoint the principal defect in metaphysical materialism is its ahistoricism. Marx's own alternative to Hegelianism therefore takes the form of a "historical materialism" rather than that of another metaphysics. Before the details of this "new materialism" can be elaborated, however, another shortcoming in metaphysical materialism must be clarified.

The foregoing account of Marx's dispute with Feuerbach provides the background for a discussion of this section's title "Metaphysics as Monistic Explanation." The title refers to Marx's belief that metaphysical theories suffer from reductionism; namely, they attempt to bring immensely diverse phenomena under a single explanatory principle. Naturally, Marx bases this blanket criticism of metaphysics on his familiarity with two specific systems— Hegelian idealism and Feuerbachian materialism. Despite the evident differences between the two brands of metaphysics, Marx feels that both commit the same sin. A brief review of previous examples will clarify the point.

Since Hegel uses mastery and slavery primarily to explicate the notion of self-consciousness, it should not be surprising that he ignores certain obvious dimensions of the relationship. To take a favorite Marxist example, Hegel glosses over the point that mastery and slavery usually does not arise between isolated individuals who are testing their worth; the relation normally arises as a social institution that reflects differences in wealth. For this reason Marx's study of mastery and slavery extends to the economic forces that generate and perpetuate the relationship. The point is not to accuse Hegel of ignorance. His failure to cover important aspects of mastery and slavery cannot be written off as either oversight or stupidity; it must be understood as a consequence of his metaphysical project. Clarification of the metaphysical notion of self-consciousness in its absolute form does not demand a full investigation of the master-slave phenomenon; hence Hegel does not offer one.

From Marx's standpoint the insufficiency of a Hegelian treatment of mastery and slavery or any other concrete phenomenon results from its attempt to reduce such a phenomenon to one more manifestation of an underlying metaphysical principle. Hegel exemplifies this reductionist tendency in that his analysis of mastery and slavery concentrates on the changes in *consciousness* that occur through the relationship. Marx does not dismiss each of Hegel's conclusions in this regard; for instance, he does not dispute that the slave's newly acquired skills enhance his self-awareness. But Marx questions whether an investigation of mastery and slavery in the concrete can overlook, say, the economic or political dimensions of the relationship. More generally, Marx concedes that Hegelianism qualifies as impressive metaphysics, but he denies that even good metaphysics provides a satisfactory explanation of reality. Hegel's penchant for monistic explanation—his inclination to reduce diverse phenomena to so many manifestations of the absolute spirit—is symptomatic of metaphysics in general; hence Marx's critique of Hegelianism transfers readily to the Feuerbachian alternative.

Although Marx sympathizes with many of Feuerbach's claims he still renounces their metaphysical character and their consequent inadequacy. Both thinkers agree that God, who has been credited with the creation of the entire material world, exists merely as a creature in man's imagination. Marx affirms Feuerbach's contention that the supposedly spiritual and transcendent deity really belongs to the material universe as a projection of human consciousness; yet this critique does not go far enough for Marx. It fails to pursue the analysis of religion by enumerating those conditions in the secular world that engender and sustain religious illusion. Marx's own attack on religion therefore includes explanations of the political function of religion; for instance, a monarch appeals to a theory about the divine right of kings in order to protect his own position. Thus it would be misleading to state flatly that Marx either accepts or rejects Feuerbach's criticism of religion. He admires Feuerbach's effort to anchor the spiritual world in a material or secular bedrock, but he laments the narrow perspective that any metaphysical explanation imposes.

Marx's case against metaphysics centers on the charge that no account of reality can be both adequate and monistic—a charge that reflects his conviction that the complexity of concrete phenomena defies every brand of metaphysical reductionism from the crudest materialism to the loftiest idealism. Marxian explanation attempts to ensure its own adequacy by covering the multiple factors that make up a particular phenomenon like mastery and slavery. The goal of adequacy dictates that Marxian theory must be comprehensive in its scope and flexible in its choice of explanatory categories. Thus in dealing with the master-slave relation Marxism considers more than the economic and political sides of the matter; it also looks at data from psychology, anthropology, religion, and other fields. Marx's belief in the irreducible complexity of reality accounts for his break with metaphysics and also underlies his distinction between ideology and science.

Ideology versus Science

A recurrent theme in Marx's demarcation of his own system from its competitors is that only Marxism avoids the confusion between reality and its theoretical reconstruction. In equivalent terms the distinction between science and its ideological caricatures reportedly marks the distance that separates Marxism from other theories.

Marx takes his primary examples of ideology from religion

and philosophy. His crudest statement of the difference between ideology and science runs as follows. Science investigates the concrete phenomena that make up the universe. Naturally, these phenomena may range from the subatomic particles studied in physics to the ordinary objects considered in botany. From a thorough analysis of the phenomena that fall within its domain a particular science derives conclusions about the laws that govern them. But science never mistakes its intellectual reconstruction of reality for the original; it remains in contact with the phenomena under investigation so that they may provide a check on both its comprehensiveness and the accuracy of its specific claims. Ideology, however, either remains oblivious to its origin as a single intellectual reflection of reality or soon forgets this crucial fact about its inception. An ideological theory detaches itself from its particular basis in reality; hence it tends to transform one aspect of intellectually reflected reality into an autonomous realm. In an extreme example philosophers such as Plato have suggested that a world of metaphysical entities lies beyond the ordinary physical universe; actually, however, such a world exists only in the minds of those who imagine it.

For the sake of emphasis and subsequent clarification the above exposition of the science-ideology distinction has simplified even Marx's most unsophisticated accounts. First, the words *science* and *ideology* designate opposite poles of a continuum; a particular theory may be either more or less ideological than another. In addition, Marx does not subscribe to a naïve empiricism with respect to the origin of science. He does not suppose that science begins with an uncomplicated act of abstraction that produces an intellectual photograph of the facts under investigation. Instead, he attributes the birth of science to a special kind of reflection on a definite kind of theory; namely, science originates as a *critique of ideology*.[18] Marx's claim that the inception of science coincides with his own attack on ideology (specifically, philosophy) helps to locate him within the history of Western thought. Although he intends to break with philosophy, Marx acknowledges it as a requisite phase in the evolution of theory toward science. Since it supposedly grows out of a critique of religion, philosophy sets the scene for the appearance of science, which emerges when the critical thrust of philosophy has been turned against philosophical thought itself. Thus science may be characterized as a critique of both religion and philosophy because its own critique of philosophy incorporates the philosophical critique of religion.

Marx's suggestion that science represents the culmination of an evolution within thought cannot claim originality; for instance, Comte's law of the *tois ètats* provides an earlier statement of the same claim. Perhaps the most interesting aspect of Marx's version is its analysis of philosophy as ideology, which can be divided into two parts. The first contains a functional explanation of ideology; the second supplements this explanation with a critical analysis.

The functional account indicates the two principal ways in which ideology relates to social classes. First, an ideology represents at a theoretical level the activity of one particular class. For instance, the philosophy of liberal (individualistic) democracy furnishes an ideological representation of bourgeois life. In promoting such ideals as the equality of all men before the law, the inalienability of certain personal rights, or the primacy of the individual over the state, this philosophy reflects a situation in which mutually independent producers and merchants compete in an open market. In simpler terms, the philosophy of liberal democracy presents an intellectual reflection of the capitalist in operation. To summarize the first link between a social class and ideology: every ideology *reflects the activity* of some social class.

Marx's claim that an ideology gives theoretical expression to the activity of a particular class does not imply that members of the class recognize their ideology as such. For instance, he insists that his own brand of socialism constitutes the proper ideology of the proletariat because it calls for liberation of the "real producers" from their capitalist oppressors; he admits, however, that most proletarians fail to appreciate that Marxism expresses their genuine interests. Thus an ideology may do more than just reflect the activity of a class; it may express the real interests of a class that remains oblivious to the fact. However, the interests expressed in such an ideology correspond to a particular class only because they reflect its activity. To continue the above illustration, Marx argues that his theory articulates the real interests of the proletariat precisely because members of the class perform the manual labor without which capitalism would collapse; hence he believes that the workers should control the system their production supports. In any case, to summarize the second aspect of the connection between ideology and a social class: every ideology *expresses the real interests* of some social class.

Two conclusions can be drawn from the claim that an ideology expresses the real interests and reflects the activity of a social class. First, an ideological dispute points to an underlying antagonism between or among the classes whose interests the conflicting ideologies express. Thus Marx regards his own disagreements with an economist like Adam Smith as an intellectual duplication of a social conflict; specifically, Smith's theory of laissez-faire economics enunciates the interests of the capitalists, while Marxism articulates those of the workers. Second, an ideology that rules the intellectual scene at a particular time probably owes its position more to the strength of its corresponding class than to its intrinsic merits. Thus the acclaim Smith's theory enjoyed during the 19th century comes more from its status as bourgeois ideology than from its cogency as a piece of theoretical economics. Naturally, the ruling ideas of a period also may deserve attention in their own right; even though Marx condemns Smith's work as an ideological reflection of the bourgeoisie, he still acknowledges its insights into capitalism.

Marx's critical analysis of ideology makes use of the functional explanation. With the alleged exception of Marxism itself, different ideologies share at least two other features. As theoretical reconstructions of (social) reality they tend to be both *fragmentary* and *ahistorical*. The special status of Marxism will be considered later; hence this discussion pertains exclusively to non-Marxian ideology.

The fragmentary character of an ideology stems from its relation to one particular class. Since it mirrors the activities and special interests of *one* class, each ideology portrays only a limited sector of the total social landscape. The example of Smith's economics again can be used for clarification. Even the abbreviated title of his principal work, *The Wealth of Nations*, indicates the well-circumscribed area of its concern—namely, the economic miracle that labor achieves under capitalism. Although this treatise may describe with accuracy the processes through which capitalism constantly transforms accumulated wealth into additional wealth, it still reflects only a restricted area of (social) reality. Marx expresses the criticism as follows.

> It is true that labor produces wonderful things for the rich, but for the worker it produces privation. It produces palaces, but for the worker hovels. It produces beauty, but for the worker deformity. It replaces labor by machines, but some of the workers it throws back to a barbarous type of labor, and the other workers it turns into machines. It produces intelligence, but for the worker idiocy, cretinism.[19]

Because it covers only a narrow sector of capitalism, Smith's theory distorts as well as reflects (social) reality. In more exact language, his theory promotes the false impression that the facts associated with the generation and accumulation of wealth offer a fair picture of capitalism as a whole. That impression must be dismissed as false because capitalism likewise impoverishes and dehumanizes. Thus an ideology simultaneously reflects and distorts (social) reality because of its fragmentary character. It reflects the activity of a particular class; hence it provides an accurate, if limited, representation of (social) reality. By its failure to encompass the full range of social activity, however, an ideology also distorts reality.

Within a particular era an ideology offers a fragmentary and therefore a distorted picture of (social) reality. But an ideology may distort the facts in another way; namely, it can present a restricted view of reality at any given time *and* across time. Bourgeois economists such as Smith tried to specify the laws that govern capitalism. In formulating the laws, however, these economists rarely included the appropriate historical qualifications. Instead of talking about economic laws during the capitalist period of history, they begin discussing *the* laws of economics. Marx therefore derides the bourgeois economists as "prisoners of the concepts of a particular phase in the development of society."[20] Another example of such ahistoricism can be drawn from Western philosophy. As one form of ideology philosophy tends to detach itself from the activity it reflects at a theoretical level. For instance, Aristotle's political theory acquires a certain independence from life in the Greek *polis*; without this independence, of course, his theory would be largely irrelevant for those of different times and circumstances. In any case by relying so heavily on jargon philosophy accentuates its detachment from the noncontemplative activity it reflects. Philosophy consequently seems to lose its roots in ordinary experience, which explains the familiar complaints about its being abstract, removed, and irrelevant. Marx states the point as follows.

> For philosophers one of the most difficult tasks is to descend from the world of thought to the actual world. *Language* is the immediate actuality of thought. Just as philosophers have given thought an independent existence, so they had to make language into an independent realm. This is the secret of philosophical language, in which thoughts in the form of words have their own content. The problem of descending from the world of thoughts to the actual world is turned into the problem of descending from language to life.[21]

Four aspects of ideology have been considered so far: first, it reflects the activity of one social class in particular; second, it expresses the special interests of one class; third, it offers a merely fragmentary picture of (social) reality at any given time; fourth, it may be ahistorical in its outlook. At least to some extent Marxism fits the first three descriptions. With its emphasis on labor, Marxism reflects the activity through which man as a worker constantly transforms the rest of nature, civilization, and himself. In calling for the workers' revolution Marxism articulates the specific interests of the proletariat. Finally, Marxism emphasizes the negative side of capitalism.

As the ideology of a suppressed class, though, Marxism cannot afford to be ahistorical. Once a class has gained a position of dominance, its ideological reflection of itself tends to become ahistorical. Except during the period of its struggle for domination, a class usually subscribes rather automatically to its own ideology because most members of a class simply lack the time and inclination to submit their ideological commitments to reflection. For instance, the typical capitalist does not question in depth whether the law of supply and demand *ought* to govern the production and distribution of commodities; he probably takes for granted the truth and the propriety of this law. Thus a class seems inclined to regard the ideological expression of its interests as a body of fixed and self-evident truths, and the inclination should become more pronounced as a class brings the rest of society under its dominion. While struggling for power, however, a class may find it expedient and even necessary to defend its ideology against that of its main rival; this defense, in turn, should place the ideology in historical perspective. An example may be instructive.

Rousseau's theory of the social contract (which states roughly that the state originates with a contractual agreement between the citizens and their rulers) helped to put the dying feudal aristocracy on the defensive by attacking its ideology of the divine right of kings. In order to mount a convincing attack against this alternative view on the origin of the state, Rousseau's theory had to be consistent, cogent, and so on, but precisely that his theory had to compete with the ruling ideology brought out its historical dimension. Rousseau's account emerges as the ideological representation of the rising bourgeoisie, the class that hopes to win full control of society *in the future.* After the bourgeoisie reaches its goal, however, its interests presumably would not be served by the suggestion that it, too, will decline. Bourgeois ideology presumably articulates the interests of its corresponding class by implying the permanence of capitalism since the bourgeoisie rule in the system.

The discussion above pointed out why a ruling class tends to inject an ahistorical perspective into its ideology. The discussion also mentioned the reason that a suppressed class tends to acknowledge the temporal or historical dimension of its ideology; namely, the interests of such a class require an end to its suppression at some future date. Thus Marxism as the ideology of the proletariat predicts the demise of capitalism and its replacement by communism, a system under which the proletariat enjoys prosperity and freedom. But the historical perspective of Marxism indicates more than its function as the ideology of the proletariat; it also shows Marxism's ambition to qualify as science.

Marxism as Ideology and Science

The privileged position Marxism claims for itself among competing ideologies derives in part from the unique mission it attributes to its corresponding social class, the proletariat. Through its upheaval of capitalism the proletariat reportedly will undermine the basis of all ideology, and the elimination of ideology will coincide with the completion of communism, the classless society. Thus Marxism is an ideology that predicts an end to social conflict and the ideological disputes that reflect it. In brief, Marxian ideology envisions and promotes the end of ideology.

As noted earlier, by articulating their conflicting interests ideology reflects the division of society into opposing groups; but to say that ideological disagreements simply mirror conflicts among classes is to suggest that those disagreements will cease once their sustaining conflicts have been resolved. If ideology springs from social division, then social reconciliation should signal its demise. Marxism predicts just such a state of affairs; namely, it forecasts a society in which men no longer will divide into opposing groups. Marxian theory therefore anticipates the circumstances in which ideology, as the intellectual reflection of social divisions and their attendant antagonisms, will disappear. This supposedly unique feature of Marxism explains how it can function as the ideology of the proletariat without being purely partisan (namely, purely ideological) in its outlook. Presumably the resolution of social conflict will benefit everyone; hence the ideology that predicts and promotes this happy situation will express the real interests of every class.

As the ideology that enunciates the genuine interests of every class Marxism escapes condemnation as a merely fragmentary representation of (social) reality. It therefore meets the minimal requirement of science; namely, it furnishes nonpartisan or *objective* knowledge. Scientific knowledge also may be characterized as *universal*. Unfortunately, however, Marx offers no adequate clarification of scientific universality. In *Capital*, for instance, he proposes to enumerate the laws that regulate capitalism and determine its destruction. The question arises whether those laws invariably govern every capitalist society or whether they hold only for most cases. Stated somewhat differently, Marx draws no sharp distinction between a scientific law as a strictly universal truth and as a broad generalization that approaches strict universality as an ideal. Marx regards science as a theoretical reconstruction of reality that has a more comprehensive scope and objective perspective than does ideology; but he fails to elaborate on the precise character of scientific universality and objectivity.[22]

Marxism differs from typical ideology because it supposedly expresses the interests of all men. The point can be summarized by saying that Marxism moves away from mere ideology in the direction of science. Even Marx does not suggest, though, that his theory qualifies as science just because it avoids a completely partisan outlook; it must meet other standards as well. First, a science must furnish an adequate causal account of (social) reality; for Marx, science thus cannot offer monistic (namely, metaphysical) explanations. Second, science must provide a comprehensive analysis of its subject matter; for Marx, science thus must be historical in its approach. These requirements will be considered in order.

Despite his formal training and enduring interest in such traditional philosophical problems as freedom, Marx gradually turned away from philosophy in his search after the appropriate categories for discussing such issues. In the early writings Marx's primary interests and his selection of jargon show the influence of both Hegel and Feuerbach. The most striking example is his analysis of *alienation*, which owes its inspiration and even much of its insight to these two thinkers; the term itself comes from them. In the later works, however, Marx relies increasingly on the terminology of economics and sociology. The shift in vocabulary warrants attention because it indicates Marx's effort to broaden the explanatory apparatus he inherits from philosophy. Thus Marx's study of freedom does not fall within a broader metaphysical analysis of, say, consciousness. Instead, the study deals directly with the economic, political, and ideological phenomena that influence the exercise of freedom.

Marx's reliance on economic categories (for instance, capital, mode of production, wage labor) has left him open to the charge that he defends an economic determinism. As discussed earlier, this metaphysical reading of Marxism draws exegetic support from the infrastructure-superstructure distinction. Marx states, for example, that the economic base of society "determines" its political superstructure. In addition, passages like the following seem to present incontrovertible evidence in favor of the metaphysical interpretation. "The hand mill gives you society with the feudal lord; the steam mill society with the industrial capitalist."[23] Although such quotations cannot be ignored, their importance must not be overrated; Marx, like most polemicists, enjoys a flashy slogan. However, such passages rarely convey his full position. He acknowledges, for instance, that an ideology (which belongs to the superstructure) may outlive its economic base; hence bourgeois philosophy may remain vital in postcapitalist society. Marx also appreciates that the state can influence its economic foundation by manipulating the supply of money, the conditions of employment, immigration, and other areas. Thus causal relations between the infrastructure and the superstructure can be reciprocal as well as unilateral.

Although Marx's penchant for economic categories cannot be construed as a metaphysics—an economic determinism—it indicates his conviction about the primacy of the material world. Marxism highlights economic factors on the grounds that man's struggle for life represents the central, but certainly not the only, fact of his history. Marxism defends the causal primacy of economics without embracing monistic or metaphysical explanations—a distinction that helps to clarify the description Marx attaches to his theory, "the materialist conception of history." As a materialism Marxism emphasizes that man's material life has on his existence a bearing far greater than his mental or contemplative life. Accordingly, Marx reserves his sharpest attacks against metaphysics for the idealistic rather than the materialistic versions, for an idealism distorts reality not only through its monistic explanations but also by giving consciousness (spirit) precedence over matter. Even though Marxism accentuates material factors, however, it does not confine itself to merely material or economic explanations. Marxism counts as a materialism only in the sense that it defends the primacy of man's material (economic) life over any other single aspect of his existence.

Comprehensiveness is the second requirement that must be met by a scientific theory, and Marxism supposedly meets it because of its historical perspective. The point can be clarified. Marxism studies man, particularly with reference to his material existence, which comprises numerous activities, the most significant involving man's struggle for survival. But the struggle rarely pits an isolated individual against the rest of nature; in different words, material life usually occurs within a social context. Marxism therefore makes society rather than the individual the basic unit of its analysis, which emphasizes the dynamic and evolutionary character of society. In sharp contrast to the bourgeois economists who play down the historical dimension of capitalism, for instance, Marxism portrays this system as the last major obstacle in man's pilgrimage to universal freedom. Its historical perspective allegedly safeguards Marxism from the partisanship that typifies other ideologies. In summary, Marxism tries to satisfy the requirement of comprehensiveness with its commitment to historical explanation.

This section has reviewed two ways in which Marx attempts to ensure the scientific quality of his theory: first, by opposing and avoiding metaphysical (monistic) explanations; second, by emphasizing the historical dimension of reality. The final section will consider Marxism as the critique of philosophy that transcends philosophical explanation while preserving philosophical ideals.

Marxism and Philosophical Ideals

As noted in the introductory section, the theme of revolution has been a source of misunderstanding with respect to Marx's dissatisfaction with Western thought. Specifically, confusion has arisen between (a) Marx's critique of capitalism and (b) his call for its abolition through revolution. The simple equation of (a) with (b), which implies that Marx wants to break with Western thought by abandoning theory in favor of (noncontemplative) action, plays down an important fact about Marx's procedure. His attack against capitalism is indirect in the sense that he raises objections against various theories about it. Marx selects theories from his favorite victims, the bourgeois economists (mainly Smith, Ricardo, and Say), the German idealists (especially Hegel), the romantic socialists

(Owen, Fourier, Saint-Simon, and others), and the social reformers (such as Proudhon); thus Marxism repudiates other theories about reality rather than theory itself. The point can be made in different terms. A preceding section mentioned that Marx describes philosophy as a critique of religion; he then characterizes his theory, which supposedly constitutes a science, as a critique of philosophy. Perhaps a more detailed exposition of these claims will help to clarify the connection between Marxism and previous Western thought.

Philosophy seeks to undermine the autonomy of religious phenomena by reducing them to philosophical phenomena. Despite its incompleteness, Feuerbach's critique furnishes the model for the philosophical reduction of religion by reducing an apparently religious fact like God's existence to the secular phenomenon of man's imagining an entity greater than himself. In short, Feuerbach subsumes religion under the philosophy of man.

Marx's critique of philosophy follows a similar pattern by incorporating philosophy into a broader theoretical framework, the "materialist conception of history." This critique traces the connection between philosophy and material life as a whole. Thus Marx views philosophy as one example of mental work that produces as its commodity various philosophies. The activity of philosophizing therefore presupposes the division of labor within society, notably the demarcation of mental from manual labor. Further, philosophers themselves belong to a distinct social class that arises from the division of labor; they earn their livelihoods as professional intellectuals (for instance, teachers). In addition, Marx claims that most of the German philosophers come from the bourgeoisie because the class affords the financial security and resultant leisure any contemplative activity requires, and that their social origin explains the abstract character of German philosophy. Since the bourgeois philosophers enjoy a relative immunity from the hassle of ordinary existence, their theories suffer from a corresponding detachment from material life.

> We have shown that thoughts and ideas acquire an independent existence in consequence of the personal circumstances and relations of individuals acquiring independent existence. We have shown that exclusive, systematic occupation with these thoughts on the part of ideologists and philosophers, and hence the systematization of these thoughts, is a consequence of division of labor and that, in particular, German philosophy is a consequence of German petty-bourgeois conditions.[24]

Marx's critique of philosophy can be described in a much briefer fashion; namely, it reduces philosophy to one kind of ideology. But his objections against philosophy do not stem solely from the conviction that it, like religion, cannot claim autonomy. Stated somewhat differently, Marx's critique does not stop once philosophy has been assimilated as ideology into his system. He attacks both the alleged irreducibility of philosophy and the philosophical treatment of specific issues such as freedom, justice, and happiness.

With regard to freedom, for example, philosophical analyses seem to arrive at one of two unacceptable conclusions. Either they present an unrealistic, romantic vision of a utopia that can be won without a political struggle, or they encourage political resignation by relegating such ideals as freedom to the realm of contemplation alone. The romantic conception of freedom inspired the often-bizarre social experiments that took place in Europe and America during the 19th century and again have become fashionable. Such romanticism poses no serious problem for Marx, however, because he regards revolution as a precondition for the liberation of man from both nature and oppressive social systems. Marx believes that communism (his version of the free society) remains impossible apart from the industrial revolution and its related social upheavals, the bourgeois and proletarian revolutions; thus he generally dismisses with derision the romantic conception of a free society. However, the pessimistic view that freedom cannot be fully cultivated in the real or noncontemplative world presents a more difficult challenge to Marx's position. This view puts him on the defensive by implying that his forecast of a classless society suffers from the very romanticism he condemns; accordingly, Marxism seems more visionary than scientific. The example of Hegel illustrates the pessimistic view.

The notion of dialectical suppression-fulfillment *(Aufhebung)* may be the most difficult in Hegelian metaphysics. A rudimentary analysis of it will be helpful here. In the *Phenomenology* the word *dialectic* designates the kind of process through which the absolute spirit approaches the ideal of perfect or unlimited knowledge of itself. The process can be described as a historical (temporal) progression that obeys strict laws. To say that the absolute spirit moves dialectically toward the goal of absolute knowledge is to claim that every stage in its movement falls under a law; hence nothing in the history of absolute consciousness happens by chance. The peculiarity of dialectical movement arises from the precise relation between any given phase within the entire process and the phases that precede and succeed it; for each moment in the dialectical progression both annihilates and preserves, both eliminates and completes, both destroys and fulfills its antecedent moment. This abstract description of dialectic can be supplemented with a clever metaphor from Hegel himself.

> The bud disappears when the blossom breaks through, and we might say that the former is refuted by the latter; in the same way, when the fruit comes, the blossom may be explained as a false form of the plant's existence, for the fruit appears as its true nature in place of the blossom. These stages are not merely differentiated; they supplant one another as being incompatible with one another. But the ceaseless activity of their own inherent nature makes them at the same time moments of an organic unity, where they

not merely do not contradict one another, but one is as
necessary as the other; and this equal necessity of all
moments constitutes alone and thereby the life of the
whole.[25]

This passage brings out the key characteristic of dialectic. Each
step in the process simultaneously advances and restricts the entire
movement. Thus the blossom advances the plant's growth because
fruit will appear only after the bud has been supplanted by the
blossom; yet the blossom likewise retards growth in the sense that
the fruit cannot appear while the blossom remains intact. Thus
the blossom completes its function of advancing the plant's growth
in the very moment of its own elimination, for its disappearance
coincides with the appearance of the fruit. Every advance in a dialectic therefore constitutes another restriction that must be overcome;
without the constant removal of such impediments, the dialectic
simply would come to an end.

This metaphorical summation of dialectic now can be applied
to the issue under discussion. A previous analysis of mastery and
slavery (in "Hegel and Marx on Metaphysics") noted that Hegel
uses the phenomenon as an illustration for the metaphysical notion
of self-consciousness. The point must be expanded here. The
relationship illuminates and represents one phase through which
absolute spirit passes in its dialectical movement toward absolute
knowledge; hence mastery and slavery can be characterized as
one moment in a dialectic. Its succeeding, supplanting, and fulfilling
moment is *stoicism*, which therefore represents another moment
in the dialectic of absolute spirit.

The connection between the master-slave relationship and
stoicism has significant political implications. Stoicism can be
described as an attitude of indifference that the self adopts toward
its position in the real world—an attitude that rewards the self by
making it relatively immune to outside disturbances. The stoic gains
a measure of freedom from his indifference because his internal

life becomes independent of his external circumstances; consequently, a master and his slave can be equally successful stoics. Yet the stoic pays for his freedom in an obvious manner. He acquires his peculiar brand of freedom only by forfeiting freedom of action; more accurately, he renounces freedom at a noncontemplative level in order to achieve it at a contemplative level.

That stoicism represents the dialectical *fulfillment* of mastery and slavery, however, appears as a confession of profound pessimism; namely, it suggests that the quest for freedom (especially on the part of the slave) necessarily ends with the renunciation of action. In more poignant terms, the slave can win the freedom for which he prepares himself with his work only by resigning himself to freedom of thought alone. Marx's objection to this pessimistic appraisal becomes clear in his regard of capitalism as the historical culmination of mastery and slavery, and he defends the thesis that the proletariat's struggle for liberation constitutes the appropriate effort at overcoming its enslavement. In short, Marx insists that real freedom can be won through revolutionary action; he therefore dismisses merely contemplative or stoical freedom as a sham.

For Marx the romantic and pessimistic views on freedom share an important feature: both lack scientific support. The romantic vision of utopia ignores the alleged necessity of revolution; the pessimistic resignation to freedom at a merely contemplative level distorts the putative fact that real freedom can be won through revolution. Marx maintains that his theory alone qualifies as scientific; its predictions concerning the demise of capitalism and the eventual appearance of a free society rest on a foundation of historical fact. If he is correct, then his theory uniquely fulfills the ambitions that have been articulated throughout Western thought, for Marxism claims to demonstrate that theories about freedom can be translated into fact through revolution. Although Marx himself did not have much success in initiating or leading revolutions, his contribution as the theoretician of revolution cannot be underestimated; he reportedly furnishes the scientific assurance that revolution can and will succeed. In summary, Marx endeavors to replace philosophical speculation on such themes as freedom with a science that specifies the manner in which revolution introduces freedom into the real world; hence Marxism is the theory that proposes and promises that such ideals as freedom need not be confined to theory. Chapter 3 attempts to evaluate the claim that Marxism constitutes a science.

3
Marx and the Utopian Finale of Social Conflict

Science and the Critique of Bourgeois Ideology

By engaging the intellectual representatives of the bourgeoisie in debate, Marx aligns his activity as an ideologist with his own theory about the origin of science, for this theory locates the genesis of science in the critique of bourgeois ideology. A short review of ideology and science should clarify the matter.

Ideology shares with science the function of presenting an intellectual reconstruction of reality. Yet an ideology also distorts what it reflects accurately; it misrepresents the total character of (social) reality precisely because it articulates the interests of one class in particular. Science, though, seeks to reflect reality without allowing partisanship to vitiate the reflection; thus it tries to gain an unobstructed view of reality as a whole. The ambition to be *objective* by being *comprehensive* dictates that science must explore the multifarious factors that comprise reality; it must attend above all to the historical dimension that discloses the dynamic, evolutionary character of reality. In summary, science breaks with ideology by placing reality in proper historical perspective, which protects it from the narrowness and corresponding prejudice that infect purely ideological theories.

Marx's etiology of science makes his own ideology an integral step in the movement from merely ideological to truly scientific thought. His polemic against competing theories reportedly promotes science by attacking bourgeois ideology in particular. Since that ideology dominated the scene during the 19th century, it and its corresponding social class then posed the chief threat to science; hence Marx's antibourgeois ideology seeks to remove the major intellectual impediment to science under capitalism. The special contribution Marx's ideology makes to the evolution of thought into science can be stated somewhat differently. Marxism has an advantage over internal critiques and improvements of bourgeois theory because of its status as the ideology of the proletariat. Since an internal critique remains within the theory it tries to amend, such a critique may become contaminated by the ideological bias associated with that theory. The case of the French socialist Proudhon illustrates the danger.[1]

Both Marx and Proudhon criticize capitalism by calling for an end to private ownership of the means of production. From Marx's standpoint, however, Proudhon's critique suffers from its piecemeal approach; it rests on the naïve supposition that elimination of private property alone will rectify the basic evils of capitalism. In different language, Proudhon suggests that a legal measure—transfer of the right over productive property from select individuals to society at large—can correct a complex social disorder. The rationale behind the suggestion is that the dissolution of private property will lead to a more equitable distribution of wealth which should meliorate the antagonism between rich and poor.

Proudhon's failure to advocate revolution, though, implies a belief that the problems that haunt capitalism can be solved without abolishing the system itself; for Marx, this implication indicates

Proudhon's tacit (if well-guarded) acceptance of capitalism. Marx, conversely, insists that nothing short of full-scale revolution will eliminate the conditions that both he and Proudhon object to; hence only Marx advocates the upheaval of capitalism through revolution. Such a revolution does not aim simply at a more equitable distribution of wealth, and it does not envision the mere reconciliation of warring classes. On the contrary, the proletariat's revolution allows the replacement of capitalism with a system in which the very issue of wealth no longer precipatates social unrest; therefore the revolution will facilitate the disintegration of classes and their attendant antagonisms. In summary, Marx believes that the evils of capitalism can be removed only by destroying the system in which they arise.

Marx's critique of capitalism strikes a revolutionary chord in contrast to the reformist tone of Proudhon's counterpart; hence it would be misleading to compare the two critiques solely on the basis of their shared opposition to private property. This example teaches an important lesson in interpreting Marx. His reliance on categories from bourgeois economics and philosophy, and his agreement with rival theoreticians on a specific point, should not distract from the uniqueness of his position. Marx intends to use the intellectual arsenal of bourgeois theory to lend support to a revolution against bourgeois society. He carefully selects weapons from that arsenal as he borrows Smith's insights into the operation of capitalism but disavows Smith's conservative and ahistorical perspective, and as he adopts the "critical and revolutionary" stance in Hegel's theory about the dialectical destruction-fulfillment (*Aufhenbung*) of reality but repudiates Hegel's metaphysical, and especially his idealist, commitment. Marx even shares the vision of the romantic socialists but derides their naïveté. Perhaps the best way to show how Marx borrows from bourgeois theory without embracing its ideology is to consider, in two steps, his analysis of capitalism. First, the original theory of alienation will be outlined; then its gradual refinement in mature Marxism will be discussed.

The Original Theory of Alienation

Marx's ability to invest an apparently dispassionate study of capitalism with a severe indictment of it may furnish the best proof of his skill as a critic. The subtlety and rigor of the indictment peak in the later works, which manage to convey Marx's indignation despite their ponderous detail and jargon. In the earlier writings Marx expresses himself with less restraint and relies more on terms from philosophy. But these differences fail to break the thematic continuity of his writings, for Marxism begins and ends with a critical analysis of alienation, especially as it appears under capitalism. As the first step in substantiating this claim it will be necessary to consider Marx's original account of alienation.

The early account seems to contain several enigmas. Alienation represents a natural yet impermanent condition. It constitutes an unavoidable phase in man's development; nonetheless, it deserves condemnation. Alienation advances evolution, but it has deleterious effects. The solution to these apparent puzzles comes from Marx's theory of history. If alienation is an inherently historical phenomenon, then both its appearance and its eventual disappearance may be natural events in history. In addition, if alienation occurs within an evolutionary process that follows laws, then its appearance becomes a requisite stage in history; if such laws dictate the ultimate removal of alienation, then its prolonged appearance retards man's development. Finally, even if alienation brings progress in the long run, its immediate effects may be injurious.

That Marx's account of alienation falls within his theory of history makes it immune to various charges of inconsistency. He can praise capitalism for its contribution to man's development, and without fear of contradicting himself he can castigate it for impeding progress. The historical character of alienation also allows Marx some leeway in his examination of it. Rather than offering a thorough analysis for each of its stages, he concentrates on alienation under capitalism on the grounds that the condition becomes most pronounced in this system. Thus he combines his critique of capitalism with his study of alienation; his polemic against capitalism centers on the topic of alienation, and his analysis of the phenomenon is concerned with its occurrence under capitalism. For the sake of brevity future reference to Marx's theory of alienation will not be qualified; it should be understood that the theory primarily concerns the capitalist variety.

In the original theory Marx divides alienation into two primary categories: the alienation of man from his product and the alienation of man from his productive activity. He then deduces two additional categories: the alienation of man from his potentialities as a generic being and the alienation of man from his fellow men. These four types will be taken in order.

The first kind of alienation covers the phenomenon in which the worker confronts his artifact as an independent and hostile entity that dominates him. Such alienation inverts the proper relationship because the worker as the creator of the product ought to enjoy the superior position. With respect to both *quantity* and *quality* the alienation of man from his product falls to its nadir under capitalism: qualitatively because the real producer exercises almost no control over the commodities he makes and, in fact, through his production increasingly accentuates his bondage to his product; quantitatively in the sense that most people under capitalism (at least during the 19th century) belong to the proletariat, the class of propertyless and therefore powerless workers.

Familiar aspects and symptoms of alienation in the first sense can be given. Under capitalism, for example, the worker as such normally does not decide what to produce; he probably influences that decision only as a consumer. But even a worker-consumer "falls under the sway of his product," for as every shrewd advertising executive knows, available commodities partially determine the consumer's future needs and demands. Further, the worker has no special claim to the commodities he produces himself. He can own them only by making a choice that remains open to everyone else; namely, he must purchase his products in order to possess them. The alienating separation of the worker from his product has a more serious side, though. The very production of commodities takes on such importance that the worker must gear his entire existence to the enterprise. Two obvious examples illustrate. The worker must conform to the pace of the assembly line. If he cannot keep up, he must be replaced; the line cannot be attuned to the rhythm of his production. The worker must live in the vicinity of either a factory or transportation lines leading to one so that he can earn a living; thus the production of commodities not only determines his behavior within the factory but also influences his life outside it. Commodities consequently acquire mastery over the worker in that their production takes priority over, say, their producer's happiness or health.

The Marxian account of man's alienation from his product must be disassociated from two popular views about the phenomenon. First, alienation cannot be equated with certain feelings of uneasiness that infect modern life. The complex and mechanized character of industrial society overwhelms many people so that they feel lost, confused, and perhaps even threatened. For Marx, however, such feelings belong among the symptoms of alienation; they cannot be identified with it. More precisely, Marx does not regard alienation as a merely psychological or emotional phenomenon; it constitutes a hard and unpleasant fact about (social) reality, at least during the precommunist eras.

The point can be clarified further with reference to a parallel that Marx draws between religious illusion and alienation from product. "Just as in religion man is governed by the products of his own brain, so in capitalist production he is governed by products of his own hand."[2] Marx's solution to religious alienation entails elimination of the conditions that engender it. Specifically he believes that misery must be cured before religious estrangement can be overcome, because religious illusion arises simply as a defense mechanism against suffering. Since religious alienation poses more than a psychological problem, Marx repudiates merely contemplative solutions to it. He attacks Feuerbach's critique that implies that enlightenment alone provides the antidote to religious alienation. A key assumption in this critique is that religious illusion will disappear once religion has been understood rationally or philosophically; hence the way to cure belief in God consists in explaining that God exists solely as a product of man's imagination. Marx disagrees strongly with this suggestion. Although enlightenment may be an initial and important step in going beyond any kind of alienation, including the religious variety, it remains insufficient. To emphasize the point Marx notes that his account of communism offers a *theoretical* solution to alienation under capitalism. This account, however, cannot rectify the actual condition that afflicts members of capitalist society; only construction of a communist system will accomplish that feat. "For transcending the *ideas* of private property, the *ideas* of communism are quite sufficient. But for transcending real private property, a *real* communist movement is required."³

Despite the claim that man's alienation from his product is a natural consequence of work in precommunist society, Marxism does not offer a pessimistic appraisal of the relationship between man and the rest of nature. Man's interaction with his environment need not be antagonistic; accordingly, Marx envisions the end of man's estrangement from, and therefore his conflict with, his product. The end of such estrangement supposedly comes with communism. Marx's optimism in this regard can be expressed with reference to the distinction between alienating labor and appropriation. The word *appropriation (Aneignung)* refers to both the process through which man brings the world under his dominion and the result of that process. Only man appropriates nature because he alone consciously imposes a design on it. The architect, for instance, appropriates nature in constructing a house because he arranges his materials with a definite purpose in mind; the bee follows no conscious plan in building its hive.⁴ Thus appropriation covers the purposive interaction with nature through which man ensures his survival and establishes his superiority.

Appropriation resembles every other natural phenomenon in that it has a historical dimension. The important point here is that appropriation assumes the form of alienating labor in historically determinate conditions; namely, man appropriates nature through his alienating work only during precommunist eras. That appropriation within a capitalist society leads to the most extreme alienation of man from his product does not imply the incorrigibility of the condition but suggests simply that appropriation will take the form of alienating labor until the demise of capitalism. To state the point more positively, man's interaction with nature need not end in his estrangement from his product; hence alienation of this type is a historical rather than an absolutely impassable phenomenon. Marx's distinction between appropriation in general and alienating labor as one instance of it safeguards his optimism about the society of the future—communism.

In dealing with man's alienation from his product Marx tries to avoid two extremes. The first reduces such alienation to a merely psychological illness that might not reflect an actual social problem. The second transforms the alienation into a permanent feature of man's interaction with his environment, an extreme that excludes hope that alienation can be overcome through social change. Marx's own views on man's alienation from his product fall somewhere between the two positions.

The second category of alienation covers the separation of man from his productive activity. Phenomena that fall under this category have received close attention in recent years. For instance, studies have been conducted on the effects of a monotonous and unchallenging job on the worker's efficiency, personality, and so forth. Marx offers this incisive description of industrial work.

> In his work, therefore, he [the worker] does not feel content but unhappy, he does not develop freely his physical and mental energy but mortifies his body and ruins his mind.

The worker thus only feels himself outside his work, and in his work he feels outside himself. He is at home when he is not working, and when he is working he is not at home. His labor is therefore not voluntary, but coerced; it is *forced labor*. It is therefore not the satisfaction of a need; it is merely a *means* to satisfy needs external to it. Its alien character emerges clearly from the fact that as soon as no physical or other compulsion exists, labor is shunned like the plague.[5]

The distinction between coerced and spontaneous work belongs to Marx's critique of labor in precommunist society. He defines work as the "appropriation of natural substances to human requirements," or as the activity through which man produces and reproduces his "means of subsistence."[6] Work may be described as a natural activity for at least two reasons. First, man normally must work in order to survive; hence he usually interacts with the rest of nature by working on it. Second, work sharpens man's skills so that he can satisfy his present needs and develop new ones; it therefore furnishes him with the means of fulfilling his potential for growth. As one of man's natural activities work should occur spontaneously or automatically. Marx believes that work will be spontaneous as long as man's circumstances do not frustrate or pervert such activity. His favorite example is that the monotony of the assembly line undermines the spontaneity of work; hence most people accept repetitive and boring jobs only because they must earn a wage in order to live. The point can be summarized by saying that much industrial labor depends on economic coercion; it does not happen spontaneously or freely.

Marx's analysis of man's alienation from his productive activity (work) has an important consequence for his doctrine of revolution. The topic deserves consideration here because his claims about the superiority of communism over capitalism have been misunderstood. Marx says that alienation will end, or at least diminish considerably, under communism. This prediction implies both (a) that the real producers or workers will control their products and (b) that their productive activity will be spontaneous. Marx's critics frequently overlook (b). One familiar criticism begins: capitalist nations such as the United States have succeeded in giving the workers broad control over their own products through such institutions as the joint-stock company. A variation of the criticism starts with the assertion that the vast increase in consumer goods and significantly higher wages together have the effect of making the worker into the master of his product; so Marx was wrong to insist that capitalism had to be eliminated before alienation would end. But Marx recognizes that the worker's plight can improve greatly through reforms within capitalism; he even remarks that the joint-stock company, a capitalist institution, represents the halfway house to communism and therefore an important step toward (a).

Yet even a fully equitable distribution of goods under capitalism would not silence Marx's call for revolution, for the kind of alienation that prevents (b) will continue until work becomes spontaneous rather than economically coerced. Stated somewhat differently, alienation cannot be eliminated unless the capitalist pattern of both consumption (distribution) and production has been radically altered. Thus improved wages, better working and living conditions, greater democracy cannot cure capitalism of its alienation; Marx regards such measures as mere palliatives unless they lead to (b) as well as (a). In summary, Marx's critique of capitalism covers more than the issue of distributive justice; it demands both that the workers share equitably in the wealth they produce and that they enjoy the opportunity to produce spontaneously.

The two primary kinds of alienation separate man from his product and his productive activity. These conditions, which supposedly peak under capitalism, cannot be ranked in terms of importance. The point deserves attention because Marx's mature works deal more explicitly with the alienation of man from his product; namely, they elaborate on the economic and political details associated with the worker's bondage to his product. Such emphasis cannot be interpreted as an indication of Marx's growing disinterest in the issue of nonspontaneous work. His commitment to revolution rests in large part on the conviction that capitalism cannot accommodate spontaneous production even if it manages to alleviate the proletariat's misery by putting the workers in control of their products. Before turning to the later refinements in the theory of alienation, however, it will be instructive to consider two other categories Marx deduces from the initial pair: the alienation of man from his potentialities as a generic being and the alienation of man from his fellow men.

The Marxian account of man's estrangement from his potentialities as a generic being extends the analysis offered for the two primary categories of alienation. The extended analysis centers on the distinction between a person as an individual and as one member of the species and draws on the notion of man as a self-conscious or reflective animal.

Each person obviously does not exhaust the potentialities of the entire race, especially those of future generations. Thus every actual man represents a very limited realization of indefinitely rich possibilities. Every individual, though, also can realize certain possibilities, and to the extent that he does he can advance the development of the species. The point can be expressed in more mundane language. Everyone can contribute to the evolution of the species by developing his abilities. Once these abilities have been developed they cease to be mere possibilities of man's evolution; instead, they automatically become potentialities that have been realized or actualized in a particular person.

Consciousness plays a key role in the process. First, an individual must reflect in order to appreciate that his own life constitutes only a limited realization of all human possibilities; hence self-consciousness first brings awareness of the distinction between (1) what man in particular *is* and (2) what man in general *can be*. Further, the evolution of the species will involve the maturation of precisely those talents that belong to man alone; namely, such evolution will be concentrated on the development of the higher powers associated with man's consciousness and will.[7] Marx summarizes these ideas by saying that each person adds to the "life of the species" when he uses his own life to develop his higher powers. Unfortunately, however, alienation precludes such development on an individual basis and therefore on a generic level as well. Under the capitalist systems of the 19th century, for example, most workers were so preoccupied with staying alive that they had little chance to develop their higher powers. The proper relationship between mere life and these powers became inverted; the workers used the abilities associated with consciousness and will in order to sustain life instead of using life in order to develop those abilities. In Marx's language, man's generic or truly human life became subsurvient to his individual or merely biological existence.

Man's estrangement from his generic potentialities also can be explained with direct reference to the primary categories of alienation. If individuals have virtually no chance to be spontaneous in their work, clearly they cannot advance the species by developing their higher powers; thus man's alienation from his productive activity implies his estrangement from his generic potentialities. In addition, individuals cannot produce spontaneously so long as they remain in bondage to the very products their coerced labor produces; hence man's alienation from his product likewise entails his estrangement from his truly human potentialities.

The second derivative category of alienation covers the antagonistic relationships between man and his fellow men. Marx offers this succint description of the phenomenon.

> If the product of labor does not belong to the worker, if it confronts him as an alien power, then this can be only because it belongs to some *other man than the worker.* If the worker's activity is a torment to him, to another it must be *delight* and his life's joy. Not the gods, not nature, but only man himself can be this alien power over man.[8]

In keeping with his polemical intent, Marx claims that man's estrangement from his fellow men reaches its apex under capitalism. Although this kind of alienation may be most obvious with respect to the conflict between the capitalist (master) and the worker (slave), it infects even relationships within the same class. Thus fellow workers may relate to one another as competitors for a limited number of jobs, while fellow capitalists may vie among themselves for the greatest portion of the market. As a system of economic competition capitalism tends to make men regard one another as either actual or potential threats. This state of affairs fails to reflect that man has a social nature, and the full development of that nature requires peaceful interaction, not just conflict, among men. Capitalism therefore reduces a naturally social animal to an aggressive egoist.

Marx's original theory of alienation centers on the insight that man's gradual conquest of nature generates social conditions that then ironically enslave him. The process reportedly culminates in capitalism. Through his nonspontaneous or economically coerced production the proletarian creates great wealth, most of which eludes him. The capitalist system also prevents most of its citizens (proletarians and capitalists) from fulfilling their truly human or generic potentialities. Finally, capitalism breeds antagonism among and even within social classes. Despite his critique of capitalist alienation Marx does not regard the phenomenon as unnatural. In order to appreciate his position one must recall that Marx's analysis of alienation falls within his theory of history. He sees alienation as an unavoidable phase in man's evolution toward communism, and he believes that capitalist alienation in particular must create the wealth without which communism remains impossible.

A short digression seems in order here. Marx never suggests that communism can match capitalism's productivity; in fact, he acknowledges that the level of *material* affluence will drop under communism. Marx still regards communism as a higher form of civilization because it supposedly permits full development of truly human, as against merely material, resources. In any case he insists that communism can appear only after the capitalist stage of history, for communism must inherit rather than generate enough wealth to sustain an industrial culture. Capitalist alienation therefore deserves condemnation only in the sense that its unnecessary prolongation impedes further development; such alienation cannot be condemned on the grounds that it should not have occurred in the first place. In different terms, capitalist alienation is anachronistic with respect to the future under communism; but such alienation is also a precondition for communism.

Let us now consider Marx's refinement of the original theory with regard to three topics: the division of labor and private property, the labor theory of value, and political and social revolution.

Division of Labor and Private Property

A fairly concise statement of Marxism is the following. Work is a prerequisite for human survival because man must produce and reproduce his own means of subsistence; nature generally refuses to support the indolent. Man's productive activity normally occurs within a social setting, and man himself may be called a social animal both because he usually lives among his fellows and, on a more profound level, because his nature varies according to the kind of society he works in. Marx even claims that man's nature is only the "ensemble" of his social relations. In any case work has ramifications far beyond the immediate interaction between man and his environment; it affects every aspect of social life, from the economic through the religious.

Marx clarifies the connection between work and civilization with several technical notions. For instance, "productive forces" constitute a major determinant of society because they influence the entirety of social life and therefore the specific content of man's nature. These forces comprise (1) the technology, however primitive or advanced, with which man transacts with the rest of nature, and (2) human labor power. Productive forces partially determine the ''mode of production'' that distinguishes one kind of society from others. Perhaps the phrase can be explained best with an example. Production under capitalism takes place through an elaborate social process in which workers exchange their ability to produce for a wage; hence the capitalist mode of production can be described as wage labor. A specific mode of production corresponds to a particular set of social relations. For instance, a system of wage labor has a distinct organization of classes; at the very least this system requires division between those who sell their ability to work and those who buy it. The existence of social classes generates antagonism; in capitalism the primary conflict arises between the proletarian or propertyless workers and the propertied capitalists. Finally, the division among classes has repercussions throughout society. An obvious example, the economically superior class probably controls the political, educational, and cultural life of the community; its values and aspirations tend to become those of society as a whole.

To summarize: productive forces partially determine a society's mode of production, which corresponds to a fairly distinct set of social relations. These relations also may be called *productive relations* because they spring ultimately from man's communal effort to produce his own means of subsistence. The most important productive relations reflect social division and antagonism.

The above account becomes even more involved once it includes a nonexpendable datum for any Marxian analysis—historical change. Marxism does more than list the determinants of society; it also explains the way these factors interact through time in producing revolutions. Marx's scheme for revolution can be outlined in the following manner. Through his productive activity man refines and augments the productive forces he inherits from his ancestors; hence technology and man's own skill tend to advance from one era to the next. But any change in productive forces strains the social fabric that surrounds that change.

The point becomes clear in reviewing the connection between

productive forces (technology and human labor power) and productive or social relations. Productive forces partially determine the mode of production, which, in turn, corresponds to a particular set of productive relations; hence those forces partially determine productive relations. As productive forces advance, however, they gradually outgrow the original set of productive relations. In slightly different terms, the specific productive or social relations for which productive forces bear partial responsibility have the tendency to ossify as the productive forces themselves continue to expand. Consequently, the original productive relations become obsolete with respect to the productive forces that initially supported them. Evolving productive forces therefore undermine the society that contains them. An illustration may be welcome here.

At the outset of the Middle Ages available technology and (human) labor power influenced the productive or social relations of feudalism, which had to be rural in the beginning, for instance, because it lacked the agricultural technology to support an urban culture. Medieval productive forces evolved constantly, though, and by the end of the Middle Ages technology and labor power had reached the level required for the transition to early industrial society. Significantly, the social development of feudalism failed to keep pace with its advancing productive forces. Such features as the lord-vassal relationship, weak central government, and the union of secular and religious authority stayed intact even after they had become obsolete with respect to improved productive forces. In more Marxian language, feudal productive relations hampered the full exercise of evolving productive forces. The absence of a strong central authority enabled each lord to levy his own taxes and to wage war almost at his discretion, causing multiple and often arbitrary taxation and nearly endless warfare, which did not provide an atmosphere in which large-scale production and international trade could thrive. Consequently, members of the inchoate bourgeoisie, independent artisans and merchants, found themselves at odds with the feudal aristocracy. The interests of the emerging bourgeoisie lay with the growing productive forces, while those of the dying aristocracy lay with the increasingly anachronistic productive (social) relations; hence the aristocracy sought to preserve its position by defending those productive relations against the new productive forces and the social class that championed them. Feudal society has its most famous setback in the French Revolution, which also marks the emergence of bourgeois capitalism as the dominant social system.

This summation of Marxism has omitted many important details that will be supplied later, but it provides the background for a look at two key notions in Marxian theory: the division of labor and private property. The notions will be considered in order.

Marx's statements about the division of labor pose an exegetic problem that can be solved by appealing to the distinction between the early and the mature works. The younger Marx suggests that the division will end under communism, but he later appears to retract this prediction in favor of the forecast that it will diminish markedly. Thus the mature works temper the optimism of the earlier writings. The point will be raised again; first, however, the deleterious effects of socially divided production must be discussed.

The principal division of labor occurs between workers and nonworkers. Other major classifications separate mental from manual, urban from rural labor; still other divisions correspond to the various occupations. Marx regards the division of labor under capitalism as the paradigmatic case because its adverse effects reportedly become most pronounced within the system. The unprecedented productivity of capitalism demands a high level of efficiency and expertise, which, in turn, depend on extensive occupational specialization. A worker presumably increases his output by first mastering and then remaining at a particular job, and may therefore perform a rather petty and uninteresting task for his entire career. Further, capitalism does not erase the gap between workers and nonworkers. A few parasitical capitalists control the immense wealth generated by the proletarians, the real producers who constitute the vast majority under capitalism (at least during the 19th century). Accordingly, only a small percentage of the population enjoys the enrichment opportunities that come with affluence.

The theme of socially divided labor translates easily into the language of alienation. For instance, the division between workers and nonworkers clearly relates to man's estrangement from his fellow men, because such division engenders the distinctions among social classes and the conflicts that arise both among and within those classes. In short, socially divided labor has socially divisive effects. The division of labor also has a bearing on man's alienation from his productive activity and from his generic or truly human potentialities. As work becomes more specialized, repetitive, and boring, it ceases to happen spontaneously; instead, it must be induced through economic or other kinds of coercion. Nonspontaneous work stifles rather than serves the development of man's truly human potentialities. Finally, the division of labor and man's alienation from his product are likewise interconnected. The proletarian finds himself in bondage to his product because his particular menial job does not allow him to regulate the production and distribution of commodities. He simply performs a specific service for a wage, while the capitalist makes the key decisions about the worker's products. The capitalist's reward takes the form of great wealth and corresponding control over society.

This sketch of socially divided production and alienation did not touch a difficult question: Does alienation cause the division of labor, or is the opposite true? The very formulation of the question foists on Marxism a dichotomy it seeks to avoid, especially in the later works. Marx acknowledges the legitimacy and even the usefulness of distinguishing between the individual and society as a whole. Yet this distinction does not indicate the connection between alienation and the division of labor; namely, alienation cannot be understood principally as an individual affliction that either causes or results from the social division of labor. The two primary and the two derivative categories of alienation furnish a classificatory system within which the adverse effects of socially organized labor can be located. The notion of socially divided labor helps to clarify each of these categories, especially with respect to capitalism, but it implies neither the primacy of alienation over the division of labor nor the converse. The language of alienation and that of socially divided production should be regarded as two different ways of talking about essentially the same phenomena. In summary, both alienation and the division of labor constitute *social* as against merely individual conditions, and they cannot be related as cause to effect in either direction.

A further question about alienated and socially divided labor remains to be asked: Will it persist under communism? Marx gives more than one answer. In the earlier writings he envisions communism as a community of renaissance men who can " . . . hunt in the morning, fish in the afternoon, rear cattle in the evening, criticize after dinner . . . without ever becoming hunter, fisherman, sheperd, or critic."[9] The point can be explained further in terms of Marx's early theory about the proletarian revolution. Previous upheavals altered only the specific mode of production in society. For instance, the bourgeois revolution introduced wage labor as the mode of production under capitalism; that is, the revolution brought about new divisions of labor. The most striking example is the factory workers' assumption of the productive activity that once fell to members of a feudal lord's retinue and to independent artisans. Thus the bourgeois revolution may be characterized as the introduction of a new division of labor within the general system of socially divided production. The proletarian revolution, though, reportedly will do more than just redistribute labor; it will destroy socially divided production itself.

> In all revolutions until now the mode of activity always remained unscathed, and it was only a question of a different distribution of this activity, a new distribution of labor to other persons, while the communist revolution is directed

against the preceding *mode* of activity, does away with *labor*, and abolishes the rule of all classes with the classes themselves.[10]

In his later writings Marx qualifies such predictions about life under communism. He admits that industrial labor must be specialized and therefore divided; hence its alienating character cannot be totally eliminated even in a communist society. This admission deserves attention for two reasons. First, it shows one way that Marx's brand of communism differs from some romantic alternatives. Rural nostalgia does not contaminate Marx's vision of the future; namely, he anticipates no return to preindustrial, agrarian society. Second, the admission indicates that the notion of leisure takes on increased significance in later Marxism. To admit that socially divided production will continue under any industrial system seems to concede that communism will inherit the problem of alienation from capitalism. In order to avoid such a conclusion it becomes necessary to explain how industrial labor can be divorced from its alienating quality, but Marx fails to offer a straightforward explanation. Instead, he states that a tremendous increase in leisure constitutes a *precondition* for a nonalienated industrial culture; presumably, however, such an increase may not be a sufficient condition for the end of alienation. Marx's reasoning on the matter seems clear enough. If alienation and occupational specialization go together, and if industrial society requires specialized labor, then the sole solution seems to be a radical diminution in the amount of time devoted to industrial work. The extension of leisure therefore appears as an industrial system's main weapon in combating alienation. Thus the later Marx evidently feels that communism's superiority over capitalism can be ensured as long as alienation and socially divided labor diminish significantly.

This discussion has tried to indicate how Marx's account of socially divided production relates to his early theory of alienation. A similar attempt is in order for his analysis of private property.

Perhaps the most familiar theme in Marx's critique of capitalism concerns the attack on private property; ironically, however, this theme also may be the most seriously misunderstood. Private property should not be confused with private possession, or an individual's statuatory ownership of something. Marx has nothing against the strictly legal institution that allows individual ownership and control of things; his opposition is directed against only private ownership of productive property or property that enables man to produce and reproduce his means of subsistence. Marx's critique therefore concerns private as against communal ownership and control of the means of production (for instance, factories and their equipment). In clarifying the critique it will be helpful to recall his views on man's place in nature.

Work is a prerequisite for survival, and it usually occurs within a social setting. The social character of man's productive activity implies, for Marx, that select individuals should not enjoy exclusive control over the means of production. That man produces as a social being dictates that this activity should be governed by the principle of egalitarianism. No one should have privileged access to the means of production precisely because such access almost ensures that the fruits of production will be inequitably distributed; for if certain individuals own and control the means of production, then naturally they will attempt to derive personal advantage from their position. Thus the legal institution of private property undermines an egalitarian distribution of wealth because it allows certain individuals to usurp control over the means of production, which properly belong to the community as a whole.

The fragmentation of society into conflicting classes can be explained with reference to private property. Social classes allegedly spring from different relations toward work. Those who must work in order to live fall into a distinct class, while those who can survive on the labor of others belong to a higher class; thus the owners and controllers of private property (namely, the capitalists) stand to the propertyless workers as masters to their slaves. That social division and the resultant conflict can be explicated in terms of private property indicates the close connection between this institution and alienation. For one, the division of society into conflicting groups can be characterized as man's alienation from his fellow men. One more example is sufficient. Since the legal distinction between those who have and those who lack productive property corresponds to the social difference between the masters and their slaves, this distinction relates directly to man's estrangement from his product. Alienation from product separates the real producer from his product in two principal ways. First, the worker decides neither what he should produce nor how his product should be distributed; these decisions lie with those who own and control the means of production. Second, the product enslaves the worker in the sense that the wealth his labor generates reinforces the very system that separates him from his product in the first place. The main share of wealth goes to the capitalists, and they naturally use it to strengthen their position of control.

Marx's account of private property poses an exegetic difficulty more serious than his analysis of socially divided production, although the two accounts constantly overlap. In the earlier writings Marx relates alienation to private property as cause to effect when he says that alienation first creates private property, which then intensifies alienation. Yet this account contravenes his commitment to both a sociological and a historical study of alienation. The matter can be clarified by considering the exact sense in which alienation might be construed as the cause of private property.

Marx's critique of private property is concerned with capitalism. Sometimes he singles out greed and competition—which he calls "the war among the greedy"[11]—as the demons behind the evils of capitalism. On this reading private property is a legal institution that results from a competitive mania in each capitalist; hence private property appears as the social expression of an *individual aberration*. Whenever Marx uses the language of psychology for his polemics, he lends support to the interpretation that capitalism's problems derive ultimately from the avarice of individual capitalists. Once such an interpretation has been coupled with the thesis that alienation initially causes private property, alienation appears primarily as a psychological or emotional phenomenon. This account, though, conflicts with Marx's explicit intention to treat alienation as a social condition rather than a merely individual problem. He makes the point in the following passage.

> Only as personified capital is the capitalist respectable. As such, he shares with the miser the passion for wealth as wealth. But that which in the miser is a mere idiosyncrasy is, in the capitalist, *the effect of the social mechanism* of which he is but one of the wheels.[12]

Other exegetic evidence militates against interpreting alienation as a psychological condition that underlies the institution of private property. Marx criticizes the bourgeois economists for assuming that capitalism uniquely accords with man's nature. Smith, for instance, suggests that capitalism springs from a congenital urge to "exchange and barter"; namely, this urge manifests itself on a social level as economic competition among individuals. The suggestion implies that man is an egoist whose nature impels him to compete with his fellow men. Marx objects that egoism must be seen as a sociologically determined and historically determinate condition, for supposedly man's egoism under capitalism will turn into altruism under communism. In any case Marx's criticism of Smith and others indicates that he does not want to trace the origin of private property back to an innate and inalterable drive such as greed or egoism.

In conclusion, two points warrant special consideration. First, the distinctions among (a) the original theory of alienation, (b) the analysis of socially divided labor, and (c) the account of private property have been made for the sake of a convenient exposition; these sharp distinctions do not arise in Marxism itself. Even the original theory of alienation contains (b) and (c), for example. On the whole, the three phenomena defy unilinear causal analyses. Thus alienation cannot be construed as either the cause or the effect of socially divided production; they are simply interrelated phenomena. It must be noted, however, that Marxism includes ambiguous and perhaps even inconsistent remarks. In at least one passage, for instance, Marx clearly says that alienation and private property relate to each other as cause to effect; but this statement conflicts with other tenets in his theory.

The second point of interest involves the different expressions for Marx's doctrine of revolution. The proletarian revolution can be characterized as the one social upheaval that either eliminates or radically diminishes the division of labor; other revolutions just create new divisions from the redistribution of workers. The proletarian revolution also can be described as the one that conquers (or drastically reduces) alienation. Finally, the proletarian revolution reportedly promotes construction of an egalitarian society by eliminating private property, an institution that enforces the demarcation of masters from their slaves.

The Labor Theory of Value

Marx's theory of history obviously concentrates on the transition from capitalist to postcapitalist society. That he titled his major work *Capital* lends emphasis to his special interest; the subtitle, *A Critical Analysis of Capitalist Production*, offers a clue about its content and approach. *Capital* contains more than a disinterested analysis of capitalism; its conclusions are highly critical. Further, the work considers capitalism in terms of its economic apparatus. Finally, *Capital* borrows both terminology and substance from bourgeois theorists. The labor theory of value may be the most important substantive item that Marx lifts from the bourgeois economists such as Smith, Ricardo, and Say. In dealing with the theory, however, little attention will be paid to the exact way he amends the principles he takes from these authors. The point of interest here concerns the critical content in his theory of value.

The labor theory of value can be summarized with the thesis that the value of a commodity equals the average amount of socially available time that must be invested in its production. A qualification must be added immediately in order to deter a serious misunderstanding. Each commodity produced under capitalism has two distinct values. First, it possesses a use value; namely, it has certain material characteristics that enable it to satisfy a definite human need. For instance, an ordinary tool, such as a hammer, has a physical composition and shape that make it suitable for satisfying man's need for, say, shelter; hence the hammer has a particular use value. Second, each commodity under capitalism has an exchange value; namely, it can be traded on the open market for a commodity of presumably equivalent exchange value. Now the labor theory of value can be stated more accurately: the *exchange* value of a commodity equals the average amount of time that must be invested in its production.

Two additional clarifications of the theory should be offered here. First, the term *production* in the above statement must be given a very broad interpretation. Thus the time required for securing, transporting, and refining raw materials counts toward the "time necessary for a commodity's production" just as much as the time spent on the assembly line. Second, the exchange value of a commodity must be distinguished from its price, although the two have a close connection. Ideally exchange value determines price, but additional factors usually have an influence. For example, the so-called law of supply and demand may cause price fluctuations that cannot be traced to corresponding variations in exchange value; and an entrepreneur's marketing ingenuity may permit him to charge an inappropriately high price with respect to an item's exchange value. Nonetheless, the exchange value of a commodity constitutes the main determinant of its price; over the long run exchange value and price should reflect each other.

The distinction between use and exchange of a commodity has a major place in Marx's critique of capitalism. Obviously the production of use values has not been confined to capitalism; from the very outset of his history man has been fashioning products to satisfy his needs. The production of exchange value, however, becomes pronounced only under capitalism, since this system alone centers on the institution of the open market. Stated somewhat differently, the exchange of commodities reaches its organizational zenith under capitalism, for this society caters to exchange with its elaborate system of credit agreements on international trade, and so forth. In earlier societies barter and exchange certainly had a place, but these activities represented only one aspect, rather than the central concern of life. Thus capitalism can be characterized as the system that aims specifically at the production of exchange value. Capitalism, though, enjoys unprecedented success in the production of use value as well. The immense wealth generated under capitalism must be measured by the number and the quality of commodities the system produces to satisfy man's needs; in short, the real wealth of capitalism comes from its production of use values. Yet the production of use value remains subordinate to that of exchange value in the sense that the capitalist does not manufacture commodities primarily for his own use or that of his employees but, instead, places them on the open market so that he can exchange them. Thus under capitalism a consumer usually cannot use a commodity until its producer has exchanged it; so exchange value dominates production under capitalism.

The capitalist's preoccupation with money provides a further indication of how exchange value comes to overshadow use value in commodity production. The capitalist endeavors to amass wealth, and his success can be gauged by the amount of money at his disposal. Since money qualifies as a commodity it, too, has a use value and an exchange value; but money has a unique position among commodities because of the peculiar relationship between its two values. The use value of money consists in its role as a medium of exchange. Under capitalism people usually exchange commodities by first converting them into money; namely, one person sells his product, then purchases another with the money received from the sale. The physical characteristics of money (for instance, its small size and light weight) make it far easier to exchange than are most other commodities. Money therefore uniquely assimilates a use value to an exchange value because its sole function is to facilitate the exchange of other commodities. For this reason Marx calls money the "crystallization of exchange value."

Part of Marx's objection against capitalism now can be brought into sharper focus. This system accentuates the production of commodities as exchange values at the expense of attending to their worth as use values. An exchange value need not be indicative of a commodity's ability to gratify an important human desire, for an exchange value reflects only the average amount of socially available time that must be spent in producing a commodity. An example may prove helpful here. That a limosine has an exchange value far higher than the food its owner consumes daily does not imply that the car has a superior use value; on the contrary, the food has the greater use value because it fulfills a more urgent need. Further, any particular item may become more desirable for its exchange value than for its use value. Thus the limosine's owner may prize it more for the status that accompanies its high price (which reflects mainly exchange value) than for its smooth ride (part of the use value).

This subordination of use value to exchange value inverts the proper relationship. Merely because a commodity embodies the specific amount of labor time that determines its exchange value does not enable it to satisfy a concrete need; only its material properties permit that. Food, for instance, satisfies hunger because of its physical and chemical composition; it does not satisfy because a certain amount of time has been spent in its production. The point can be summarized by saying that a commodity's use value *should* be its most desirable feature, for a commodity *normally* satisfies a need because of its use value.

This statement must include the words *should* and *normally* in order to account for the special case of capitalism. Under this system man's desire for exchange value begins to dominate his interest in use value. The change manifests itself as the quest after wealth for its own sake, and it has several familiar results. For example, the immediate goal of capitalist production ceases to be the satisfaction of specific needs. Items with the highest exchange value, rather than those whose use value makes them especially worthwhile, lay first claim on society's productive forces; hence inordinately many of the commodities under capitalism may fall into the luxury class. Greed becomes a dominant emotion, and a person may be judged primarily by his wealth. The condition reaches an extreme when society produces in order to make itself wealthier instead of happier.

The critical conclusions Marx draws from the distinction between use value and exchange value accord well with the original theory of alienation. Two examples should be enough to illustrate the point. The capitalist's preoccupation with exchange value can be described as a mania for the merely quantitative expansion of wealth. This preoccupation therefore intensifies man's estrangement from his productive activity, and it stifles rather than facilitates development of his higher powers. The two kinds of alienation will be taken in order.

Once the capitalist's primary goal becomes the endless accumulation of wealth, he naturally seeks to expand his production of commodities, usually in one of two principal ways. First, he may increase the amount of time his workers spend in production; for instance, he could start operating night and day. However, by keeping the same workers at nonspontaneous activity or by hiring new help, the capitalist simply promotes the worker's alienation from his productive activity. Second, the capitalist may make his operation more efficient with automation. Yet the introduction of additional machinery into the productive process leads to further divisions of labor and even more mechanistic kinds of work; in short, increased automation usually makes the worker's activity even less spontaneous and satisfying than before.[13]

An inordinate concern with exchange value also impedes the maturation of man's higher powers. The criticism can be clarified by recalling the definition of work as purposive and productive activity. Such activity should accommodate man's present ability to be a spontaneous and creative producer, and it should satisfy his current needs for commodities; but work also should develop man's needs and enhance his capacity to fulfill them. Thus the capitalist whose affluence protects him from the usual worries of life should have quite different needs and abilities than, say, a Roman slave. The point can be summarized by saying that man's productive activity should promote the *qualitative* development of both his needs and his capacity to fulfill them. A fixation with exchange value interferes with such development. By devoting his energies to amassing wealth, man loses the opportunity to pursue those other possibilities that arise once a certain level of affluence has been reached. In brief, the lust for wealth eventually becomes more a barrier than a means to the development of man's needs and abilities.

Because Marx condemns the preoccupation with exchange value that infects capitalism, he naturally envisions a different kind of concern under communism. His early writings in particular suggest that life under communism will be esthetically rather than economically oriented; thus he implies that production and consumption under communism will be governed by the use value instead of the exchange value of commodities.

After inheriting the labor theory of value from the bourgeois economists, Marx augments his legacy with an analysis of surplus value. His account applies the distinction between use value and exchange value to labor power itself and, with respect to economic theory, provides the most technical formulation he gives to his critique of capitalism. His analysis of surplus value is outlined below.

The statement that labor power falls within the distinction between use value and exchange value can be abbreviated by saying simply that it is a commodity, for every commodity under capitalism has both values. As a commodity labor power represents an exception to the rule of equal exchange that governs other commodities. It enjoys this special position for two reasons. First, labor power can be transformed into exchange value because of its use in the production of commodities that have that value. Second, the (proletarian) worker in whom labor power resides as the capacity to produce does not own any means of production; hence he must produce for someone else in return for his wage. In summary, the intrinsic character of labor power as the potential for producing other commodities with exchange value and the social condition of the laborer as a propertyless worker combine to make labor power an exception to the rule of equal exchange. This complicated summation can be clarified further with the aid of an example.

Of the total time a worker spends in producing commodities only a certain percentage must be set aside for meeting his wage; in equivalent terms, the worker's wage can be derived from the exchange (sale) of a limited number of the commodities he produces. The point now can be expressed with reference to surplus value. The laborer exchanges his labor power for a wage; hence his wage indicates the exchange value of his labor power. The use value of labor power comes from its role in the production of other commodities; namely, the capitalist uses labor power in producing those other commodities that he then exchanges (sells). But the total exchange value of the commodities the worker produces far exceeds the exchange value of his labor power; in short, the worker's wage does not equal the full exchange value of the commodities he makes. Thus labor power has a use value that generates an exchange value in excess of its own exchange value. The difference between (a) the exchange value of labor power as represented by the worker's wage and (b) the total exchange value of the products that result from the capitalist's use of labor power is (c) what Marx calls surplus value.

Labor power is the only genuine bargain in an open market because it alone consistently breaks the rule of equal exchange. In more Marxian language, labor power constitutes the sole commodity whose use value generates an exchange value in excess of its own exchange value, for, to repeat this crucial point, the composite exchange value of the worker's products exceeds the wage that reflects the exchange value of his labor power. Thus the worker's exchange and the capitalist's use of labor power together create surplus value, or the value the capitalist receives without having to exchange anything for it.

It must be emphasized that Marx's critique of capitalism does not concern the mere creation of surplus value. Specifically, Marx has nothing against a *free* exchange in which one person relinquishes his productive ability to another who then uses the purchased labor power in creating surplus value. If the worker voluntarily exchanges his productive ability for a wage, then the capitalist has every right to the surplus value that results from his subsequent transformation of that labor power into other exchangeable commodities. Evidently, however, the worker has no real option in the sale of his labor power to the capitalist because, since he neither owns nor controls any means of production, he must depend on his wage to sustain life. Obviously he cannot detach himself from the labor power he exchanges for that wage; in effect, then, the worker must sell himself to the capitalist in order to live. Thus the proletarian's sale of his labor power appears both coerced and enslaving.

Further, the very creation of surplus value strengthens the system that forces the worker to exchange his productive capacity in the first place. The capitalist normally invests his accumulated surplus value so that eventually it will yield even more surplus value; as a result, his wealth and consequent control over the proletarian increase. The phenomenon can be depicted in much more familiar language. Instead of using his profits for merely personal enjoyment, the shrewd businessman tries to make his wealth productive through investment. Perhaps he will expand his operation by hiring more help; then the new wealth that flows from his expanded business will increase his control over society, especially the proletariat.

The way the creation of surplus value reinforces the capitalist's position can be explained further by reflecting on two key terms in Marx's theory of value—capital and wage labor. Marx borrows from the bourgeois economists the idea that capital represents control over labor. This definition implies that the word *capital* means more than wealth; it must be understood in a sociological sense as wealth that brings control over a certain group in society (namely, those who sell their labor power). Strictly speaking, wealth becomes capital only after it has been changed into machinery (constant capital) and wages (variable capital). To summarize, wealth qualifies as capital if and only if it has been transformed into a productive force, since machinery and labor power are the chief productive forces. The relationships among labor power, surplus value, and productive forces now must be investigated in greater detail.

Surplus value has its origin in labor power, which alone can be used for producing other commodities whose composite exchange value exceeds labor power's own exchange value; surplus value equals precisely the difference between the exchange value of labor power and that of the commodities that result from its use. Consequently, labor power can be characterized as the ultimate source of surplus value. Accumulated surplus value usually remains within the productive process under the guise of additional capital; namely, the capitalist normally transforms acquired surplus value (roughly his profits) into more machinery and wages so that he can increase his production of surplus value. But capital is simply wealth that has been changed into a productive force; hence accumulated surplus value usually stays within the productive process as a new productive force. Now the relation between labor power and productive forces can be brought into sharper focus. As the ultimate source of surplus value (which eventually becomes a new productive force), labor power is the one productive force that generates additional productive forces. Thus the capitalist economy can be described as the process that transforms (1) labor power as an available productive force into surplus value, (2) accumulated surplus value into machinery and wages for the purchase of more labor power, (3) newly acquired labor power into surplus value, and so on.

Despite the key role labor power plays in capitalism, the laborer himself derives only minimal benefits from his creation of surplus value. Since he owns no means of production the laborer may not benefit at all from transformation of his labor power into new productive forces; these forces also come under the capitalist's control. Thus, that the propertyless worker must sell the only commodity he owns from the outset—his power to produce other commodities —condemns him to the lowest stratum of society. This state of affairs seems both ironic and pathetic because the real producer of surplus value finds himself increasingly removed from the enrichment opportunities that accrue to those who control the wealth he produces.

Marx's account of how capitalism increases its productive forces by converting available labor power into surplus value and capital should be read as an extension of his remarks on alienation. For instance, the transformation of the worker's productive ability into additional productive forces over which he has little control also can be described as man's alienation from his product. The social predicament that forces the propertyless worker to sell himself to the capitalist by exchanging his labor power for a promised wage illustrates man's estrangement from his fellow men. Comparable examples could be given for the two remaining categories of alienation. The important point, however, is that the theory of surplus value merely refines and extends the original account of alienation.

In concluding this section it may be instructive to consider two aspects of capitalism that indicate its alienated condition. First, capitalism can be described as the system that marshals its productive forces (both human and nonhuman) for the creation of surplus value. The institution of private property, the division of society into propertyless workers and propertied capitalists, the status of the worker's power to produce as his sole disposable commodity, the conversion of labor power into capital for the acquisition of more labor power and machinery—all conspire in the production of surplus value. Yet such value really is *superfluous*. The point becomes clear once the connection between surplus value and exchange value has been brought back to mind. As noted earlier, the mere production of exchange value hampers rather than helps the (qualitative) development of man's needs and powers. This kind of production simply caters to the insatiable greed of those who pursue wealth for its own sake; and the need for still more wealth allegedly represents the dominant characteristic under capitalism. The drive to amass wealth reaches its extreme under capitalism because the system encourages it. The preoccupation with wealth acts as a deterrent against the emergence of new interests and abilities in man.

Marx's claim that an inordinate concern with exchange value impedes man's development translates easily into the language of surplus value, which is a particular amount of exchange value. Specifically, surplus value equals the difference between the exchange value of labor power and that of the commodities such power can produce. Since the acquisition of surplus value for its own sake frustrates rather than serves man's development, the time capitalism invests in the creation of such value may be called *superfluous* labor time; by a simple extension of meaning, surplus value may be condemned as *superfluous* value. The production of surplus value is necessary and respectable only to the extent that it furnishes the economic basis for the maturation of man's higher powers. That is, the legitimacy of capitalism as the system that creates surplus value ends once the level of affluence required for communism has been reached.[14]

The second point for consideration concerns Marx's views on the "fetishism of commodities." His account fits into the theory of alienation by explaining how the production of commodities under capitalism promotes mystification and illusion, which, in turn, contribute to alienation. The notion of fetishism comes from the study of primitive religion and refers to the phenomenon in which man first attributes a magical power to certain entities (real or imagined) and later begins to believe that this power resides in the entities themselves. Ordinary superstition presents a familiar case in point; witchcraft and magic furnish more serious examples. Marx's views on the matter can be clarified with reference to the related notion of reification.

The production and circulation of commodities actually involve relationships among human beings, for men plan, produce, distribute, and consume those commodities. But productive relations tend to become detached from their basis in human interaction. In another metaphor, such relations develop their own momentum, and as they gain independent movement productive relations start to determine (as against merely reflect) man's behavior. Perhaps a cliché about money will help to illustrate the point. People sometimes suggest that money speaks, an allusion to the well-known fact that a discreet donation can be the best way of securing a favor. This truism confirms that humans have clear but often unspoken procedures for dealing with one another. These procedures may begin to dominate human interaction in the sense that people become compelled to follow them; in some countries, for instance, bribery has become an unavoidable ritual. In the language of reification, social relationships acquire relative independence; they start to resemble things that do not depend on man for their existence. Reified social (productive) relations cease to be mere reflections of how men interact; they become independent fixtures in the social environment.

Reification covers the process through which social relations assume a position of independence and dominance with respect to the concrete human beings whose interaction creates such relations in the first place. Fetishism covers the related phenomenon in which man mistakenly ascribes an independent and even superior position to the social relations that through reification control his behavior. Fetishism results from inadvertent self-delusion. Man incorrectly assumes that productive (social) relations stand beyond his control, and this assumption generally goes unchallenged. Human beings therefore fail to recognize, or tend to forget, that their own behavior supports such relations. In an obvious example, the bribery of an official could not occur unless men offered and accepted money in return for favors. It must be emphasized that fetishism does not afflict just isolated individuals. Although it concerns the psychological or intellectual dimension in man, fetishism is a social condition for at least two reasons. First, it originates with man's interaction with his fellow men; obviously fetishism about social (productive) relations could not exist without such relations. Second, fetishism infects society as a whole; the individuals who escape its mystifying effects represent an exception to the rule. At this stage of the discussion an example of fetishism should be considered.

Under capitalism commodities change hands on the open market, and the law of equal exchange may be said to govern such transactions. Since the exchange of commodities lies at the basis of the capitalist economy people easily fall prey to the fallacy that commodities themselves interact; people begin to assume that commodities obey the law of equal exchange in much the same way that physical objects obey the law of gravity. In reality, of course, *men* exchange their commodites according to laws *men* have fashioned; hence men can alter those laws under, say, communism. The belief that commodities enjoy an economic life of their own amounts to fetishism because commodities are only the objects rather than the instigators of exchange. Instead of recapitulating the above points, it might be better to consider Marx's own description of fetishism.

> The social relationships of the producers to the sum total
> of their own labor presents itself to them as a social relation,
> not between themselves, but between the products of their

labor. . . . To find an analogy, we must enter the nebulous world of religion. In that world, the products of the human mind become independent shapes, endowed with lives of their own, and able to enter into relationships with men and women. The products of the human hand do the same thing in the world of commodities. I speak of this as the *fetishistic character* which attaches to the products of labor, so soon as they are produced in the form of commodities.[15]

This analysis of use value, exchange value, and surplus value has indicated how Marx refines and extends his insights in the original theory of alienation; the point deserves emphasis because his critics as well as his supporters have been misled by his failure to retain in his theory of value much of the philosophical jargon from the earlier writings. Now let us turn to Marx's utopian predictions about the end of the condition.

Political and Social Revolution

The foregoing sections have considered Marx's critique of precommunist society, particularly capitalism. The discussion now must concern his claims about the advent of communism, with emphasis on the utopian content of those claims.

Several descriptions of communism already have received attention. It may be characterized, for instance, as the system that eliminates or at least radically reduces alienation. Communism also can be called the classless society because it heals (or significantly eases) the social division of labor, which lies at the origin of mutually antagonistic classes. In this section, however, communism will be examined with reference to the kind of revolution from which it emerges.

Marx's thesis that man is the ensemble of his social relations implies that alterations in human nature occur as changes in civilization (society). The history of revolution marks the main changes in social organization and human nature; hence history, man's nature, society, and revolution are closely intertwined phenomena, and their interrelationships should be discussed.

A genuine or *social* revolution has reprecussions throughout society. More precisely, such a revolution annihilates one society and replaces it with a different kind. A social revolution must be distinguished from a (merely) political revolution, or one that occurs within a system without causing its destruction. A political revolution takes place when one faction within society manages to establish its hegemony by wresting power from the old rulers. This action need not result in total transformation of society; the new leadership may revert to roughly the same programs as those of the group it deposed. A familiar case in point is one military junta's replacement of another. Usually these coups do not lead to radically new policies but often degenerate into a simple transfer of power and privilege between two cliques. Anyway, a political revolution does not ensure the transformation of society. This point has an important implication in Marx's theory of communism. He holds that political revolution plays an integral role in every social revolution, including communism's replacement of capitalism; yet he denies that political guarantees social revolution. In different words, a political revolution constitutes a necessary but not sufficient condition for a social revolution. The matter can be clarified further with reference to the demise Marx predicts for capitalism.

The transition from capitalist to communist society has at least three distinct phases. In the initial stage the proletariat seizes power from the bourgeoisie. This stage cannot be circumvented because the appearance of communism first requires the disappearance of capitalism, and the destruction of capitalism remains impossible as long as the bourgeoisie retain a position of dominance over the proletarians. Marx calls the second phase the ''revolutionary dictatorship of the proletariat.''[16] After ousting the bourgeoisie from power, the proletariat assumes political control of society; then it seeks to eradicate the vestiges of bourgeois influence by doing away with, say, religion. But the proletariat's dictatorship does not coincide with communism. The very exercise of dictatorial power indicates the presence of antagonistic groups within society. Since communism reportedly will be classless it cannot be confused with any system in which one class dominates. That is, a system in which the state stands in opposition to other social elements cannot be communist, for the state's existence as the political apparatus with which one part of the citizenry opposes the rest implies that society still breaks down into conflicting classes. Thus a society such as contemporary Russia, where the state has not yet "withered away," does not qualify as communist in the strict sense. Communism as the final stage in the revolutionary movement away from capitalism will be reached only after private property, the state, the conversion of labor power into surplus value, and other indicators of social division and alienation have been eliminated. The important point here, however, is that the proletarian political revolution cannot be equated with the social revolution that occurs with the completion of communism; the workers' seizure of power from the bourgeoisie marks just the initial phase in a far more extensive social change.

The importance Marx places on political revolution cannot be underestimated just because he distinguishes sharply between it and social revolution. A major difference between Marxism and romantic accounts of communism concerns the issue of political action. Marx and the romantics agree that communism furnishes the cure for alienation, but only Marx insists that a political struggle, which may culminate in bloodshed, must be included in the price of the cure. Marx rejects the idea that capitalism can evolve peacefully into a higher civilization, with internal reform providing the impetus behind the evolution. He saves his strongest vituperation for those who suggest that utopia can be secured apart from the suffering of a proletarian political revolution.

Marx's theory of social revolution becomes less grandiose as his vision matures. The earlier writings characterize the history of such revolution as man's long pilgrimage toward the promised land of freedom, equality, and justice, a journey that ends only after the proletarian revolution, which initiates the last great social upheaval before the millenium. These writings also reveal Marx's roots in Western philosophy. He says, for example, that communism represents the "realization of philosophy" because it implements the ideals that have been both fashioned in and confined to philosophical contemplation. The later Marx does not dispense with allusions to philosophy, although he relies less heavily on them. To take only one example, in *Capital* he borrows from German metaphysics the distinction between the "realm of necessity" and the "realm of freedom," and he uses the distinction in order to map the distance that separates precommunist from communist society. The matter can be explained in the following way. In the societies that antedated capitalism man inhabited the "realm of necessity" principally because of his struggle with the physical environment; metaphorically, nature forced man to work for his life. During the capitalist phase in history, however, nature finally comes under man's dominion, but man remains in bondage. The proletarian, for instance, finds himself coerced to sell his labor power for a wage, and the capitalist becomes the vassal of the greed society instills in him. Communism supposedly completes the emancipation of man. It introduces the realm of freedom by liberating man from such evils as avarice and alienating labor, which still fetter him under capitalism.

Although both the early and the mature works use philosophical materials in discussing communism, the methods differ. The earlier accounts offer specific predictions about life under communism; for example, reference already has been made to Marx's forecast about communism as a community of renaissance men who pursue numerous avocations. The later works furnish little positive detail; instead, they concentrate on the *preconditions* for a communist system. Thus *Capital* emphasizes that a radical increase in leisure, resulting from a corresponding reduction in the time devoted to noncreative and nonspontaneous production, must take place before man can enter the realm of freedom. Such institutions as private property and the political state also must be razed in the construction of a communist society. *Capital,* however, fails to elaborate on how the newly acquired leisure will be spent by men who no longer suffer from the severe alienation of capitalism. This work offers only the general prediction that communism will be esthetically rather than economically oriented, and that the evils that beset capitalism will be eliminated or at least drastically reduced.

This section has sketched the relationship between merely political and social revolution. The topic will become significant in the last section because the proletariat's seizure of power is reportedly a necessary if insufficient step toward communism, and a more detailed study of the proletarian revolution should provide the basis for a critique of Marx's romanticism.

The Human Element in the Proletarian Revolution

This section's title has a peculiar ring because the word *proletarian*, which designates a specific group of men in capitalist society, makes mention of the human element in their revolution seem redundant. The distinction between the human and non-human factors in the proletarian revolution must be drawn, though, in order to show a serious shortcoming in Marxism, but first a preliminary clarification of the distinction is necessary.

Marx's analysis of social revolution can be outlined as follows. Every society develops the "productive forces" it inherits from previous generations of (human) labor. These forces comprise both the technology and the (human) labor power society uses in production. As productive forces expand, however, they strain the fabric of the society that contains them, and eventually the fabric tears, releasing these forces for construction of a new society that can more adequately accommodate them. A favorite example is useful here. The tools and workers for mass production became available during the late medieval period, but these emerging productive forces also rendered the feudal system obsolete because it was agrarian and rural rather than industrial and urban; hence the new productive forces laid the foundation for merchantile capitalism, a system that could take better advantage of their potential. Although the transition from one kind of society to another presupposes a development in technology, such development alone cannot accomplish a social revolution; concurrent progress in the political —or strictly human—realm also becomes necessary. Capitalism could not replace feudalism without the revolutionary action of the bourgeoisie. The French Revolution provides the standard example of how one social class's political struggle complements technological progress in initiating a social revolution. Thus the origin of capitalism must be traced to both the struggle of the bourgeoisie against the feudal aristocracy and the so-called Industrial Revolution that made medieval production anachronistic.

The thesis that productive forces gradually outgrow the productive (social) relations that surround them serves as the first principle in Marx's argument about the inevitable demise of capitalism. This argument should be read as part of his more embracing doctrine that every society contributes to its own destruction in two closely related ways. First, a society develops its technology to the extent that it ironically becomes the chief obstacle against the proper use of this technology. Second, a society engenders a class whose eventual rise to power brings down the system. For capitalism Marx tries to fill in the empirical detail on each point. He attempts to predict how the increased industrialization and productivity of the capitalist economy will lead to the death of capitalist society; and he seeks to explain how the political ascendancy of the proletariat will culminate in the upheaval of capitalism. These topics will be taken in order.

Marx's predictions about the recurrent economic crises that will grow in severity until they finally shatter capitalism have been subjected to criticism from modern economists.[17] A defense of Marx on these matters far exceeds both the scope of the present study and the competence of its author, but one remark must be offered in Marx's behalf; namely, the thrust of his forecasts about the end of capitalism can be defended independently of the forecasts themselves. Perhaps the point will become clearer by recalling that Marx characterizes capitalism as the system that creates surplus value. The creation of such value actually amounts to the transformation of labor power into commodities whose composite exchange value exceeds the exchange value of labor power. Thus the *creation* of surplus value may be described with greater accuracy as the *conversion* of labor power into such value.

Marx recognizes that commodity production evolves throughout the history of capitalism; he appreciates specifically that the system increasingly replaces "variable capital" or labor power with "constant capital" or machinery. This trend toward automation affects the entire capitalist system. Since capitalism is the kind of society that seeks the greatest possible conversion of labor power into surplus value, even a relative diminution in this conversion will profoundly alter the system. If a capitalist society uses less than all of its available labor power, then it falls short of meeting its potential in the creation of surplus value. Thus even a relative decrease in the production of surplus value tends to make such a society less capitalistic—namely, less devoted to the fullest possible conversion of labor power into surplus value.

The point also can be expressed in terms of automation and leisure. The capitalists who compete with one another in the open market naturally try to improve their chances of success by running efficient operations. One way to gain a competitive edge involves substitution of a more productive machine for a less productive man, but mechanization disrupts the capitalist system because it brings a relative decrease in the use of labor power, the sole commodity that can be converted into surplus value. Any diminution in the use of available labor power entails a corresponding liberation of workers from the alienation that attends the use of their labor power for nonspontaneous jobs, and increased leisure for those workers represents a primary reward of their liberation. This gain in leisure can be described in a more technical fashion. Capitalism initially devotes more of its totally available labor time to (a) alienating work than to (b) leisure. Automation decreases the ratio between (a) and (b) because it lessens the use of *human* labor power with respect to its automated substitutes; automation therefore diminishes the relative amount of time men must spend at alienating labor. Finally, the relative extension of leisure at the direct expense of alienating work moves civilization from the precommunist "realm of necessity" toward the communist "realm of freedom."

At this stage in the discussion it seems prudent to anticipate a serious misunderstanding. Elimination of surplus value from the productive process does not mean an end to the benefits of industrialization. The point becomes clear in light of the distinction between exchange value and use value. The creation of surplus value requires the production of commodities as exchange values, for, again, surplus value is simply the difference between the exchange value of labor power (as indicated by the worker's wage) and the composite exchange value of the commodities that such power can be used to produce. However, a society's standard of living cannot be measured merely by the amount of exchange value its economy generates; in different words, the quantity of surplus value a society derives from its conversion of labor power does not indicate its real wealth. Genuine affluence can be calculated only in terms of a society's success in satisfying and developing man's needs. Thus the real wealth of a society depends directly and exclusively on the collective use value of the commodities at its disposal; for use value designates just those material attributes of a commodity that enable it to fulfill and expand man's needs.

In contrast to use value, surplus value by itself lacks the capacity to satisfy and develop a need; hence surplus value can be characterized as superfluous. Even the capitalist's efforts to create surplus value do not gratify his avarice but merely enhance his need for more wealth and in this way stifle fulfillment and development of other, especially higher, needs. Thus elimination of surplus value should not be seen as a loss; no drop in the standard of living results so long as the production of commodities as use values continues at the same pace. In slightly different language, the destruction of capitalism as the system that creates surplus value does not imply an end to material wealth. Marx nevertheless predicts that the level of affluence will fall once the mania for the endless expansion of surplus value has been cured under communism. He bases this prognosis on the insight that the quest after surplus value acts as a stimulus for the production of commodities as use values. The anticipated drop in material wealth, though, supposedly will be offset by the enrichment that results from the maturation of man's higher powers.

The preceding discussion has sketched the way increased auto-mation ironically undermines the distinguishing preoccupation of capitalism—the creation of surplus value. The main topic for con-sideration, however, concerns the second factor in the supposedly ineluctable demise of capitalism—the political revolution of the proletariat. Marx's account of the matter demands close attention because it may be the most blatantly utopian part of his theory. Before considering this account, however, it will be useful to outline some other utopian elements in Marxism.

The proletariat's struggle with the bourgeoisie reportedly initiates the last great social revolution. This revolution reaches its completion under communism, a system whose classless structure precludes the occurrence of another social revolution. Communism enjoys immunity from internal disintegration because it eliminates the tension between expanding productive forces and constricting social (productive) relations. The point can be clarified. Productive forces (both machinery and labor power) tend to outgrow the society that contains and constrains them; the resultant conflict between these forces and an increasingly obsolete social system sets the scene for revolution. Specifically, those social (productive) relations that reflect distinctions among classes impede the expansion of productive forces. Since the ruling class would forfeit its position if the development of productive forces were allowed to undermine the existing order, it naturally tries to control the expansion of such forces. Part of the control consists in suppressing the class that champions liberation of those productive forces through construction of a new society. Thus the existence of social classes acts as an impediment to the peaceful development of productive forces.

At this point Marx's views on the origin of social classes must be recalled. He insists that such classes spring ultimately from the division of labor; so the difference between the powerless and the powerful corresponds to the division between those who must sell and those who can buy labor power. Members of the ruling class, therefore, rarely must engage in manual labor. But if communism has no socially divided labor it should lack the corresponding social classes, including the class that might prevent full development of productive forces. Elimination of social classes under communism therefore removes the fetters that once constrained productive forces; so with no deterrent to their continuous expansion such forces no longer promote revolution. In summary, communism as the classless society supposedly will be free from the threat of internal disintegration.

Marx's predictions about communism can be attacked as utopian on several more counts. For one, the promise that the "revolutionary dictatorship of the proletariat" will dismantle itself after fulfilling its mission borders on the worst kind of naïveté. Marx also may be guilty of wishful thinking in supposing that the elimination of socially divided labor will mark the end of classes and the conflict among them. Differences in interest, talent, or even conviction may furnish a blueprint for social division and unrest once economic differences cease. Finally, Marx's early vision of communism as a community in which each person freely pursues various avocations seems quite romantic. Predictions about communism, however, have the same dubious advantage as every other forecast; namely, as claims about the future they cannot be refuted at present. No society to date meets the standards Marx sets for a (nonprimitive) communist society; hence no counterexamples to his vision can be assembled today. Modern China, for instance, lacks the industrial foundation Marx deems necessary for a truly communist society, and the nations of Eastern Europe appear entrenched in the transition period between capitalism and communism because the state still has failed to "wither away." Naturally, lack of evidence against Marx's forecasts cannot be construed as support for them; at the very best, absence of decisive proof remains neutral in determining the truth of any claim. For the moment, however, Marx's portrayal of communism will be given the benefit of the doubt. Instead of criticizing his utopian claims about the *social* revolution that the proletariat sets in motion, the ensuing discussion will concentrate on his romanticism with respect to the proletariat's *political* revolution. This emphasis should be fruitful because Marx's forecasts about how the propertyless workers will engineer their own emancipation can be checked against data far easier than can his predictions about the eventual outcome of this emancipation.

The slogan stating that the special interests of the proletariat coincide with the real interests of all men has become a mainstay in Marxist propaganda. By liberating themselves from the bourgeoisie, the proletarians reportedly will open the door to the realm of *universal* freedom; hence they begin to free both themselves and their oppressors when they destroy capitalism. Unfortunately, however, Marx has too little to say about how the proletariat will become aware of *even its own interests*, and he insists that without such awareness the class does not become an actual threat to capitalism. The point can be stated with greater precision.

Unlike the socialists who promise a peaceful transition to the postcapitalist era, Marx argues that the transition requires a political and possibly bloody proletarian revolution. In contrast to such disciples as Lenin, he maintains that the proletariat as a whole rather than just its leadership must become enlightened about the need for a revolution before it can succeed in making one. But Marx's analysis of the conditions in which the proletariat exists ironically lends support to the thesis that it will remain ignorant of its real interests; hence his analysis offers evidence against his own predictions of a proletarian revolution. For instance, Marx points out that the bourgeoisie try to consolidate their position of power by denying proletarians access to the means of upward mobility (for example, education). He also says that because the dominant ideology in a society normally promotes the interests of the ruling class, the proletariat will be subjected to propaganda that condemns any disruption of capitalism (for instance, moral injunctions against violence). His study of alienation concludes that long hours of nonspontaneous labor drain the worker of both physical and intellectual resources. This study also indicates that competition for jobs, housing, and so forth within the proletariat have a divisive effect so that minor disputes among themselves may distract the proletarians from dealing with the "real enemy," the capitalists. Finally, Marx emphasizes that the bourgeoisie control legal and other institutions with which they can manipulate and constrain a subservient class.

The issue of whether Marx gives an accurate survey of capitalism, especially modern versions of the system, cannot be settled here. The main point is that Marx himself enumerates major problems that may prevent the proletariat from understanding its condition, developing viable programs for improvement, and organizing politically to carry out those programs. Thus Marx himself lists some of the factors that threaten the proletariat's enlightenment and consequent political action.

The topic under discussion can be approached from another direction. Chapter 2 mentioned that Marxism claims to be the ideology of the proletariat, although its author has the credentials of a bourgeois intellectual. Marx appreciates the peculiarity but appoints himself spokesman for the proletariat partially on the grounds that most proletarians cannot recognize their own real interests. He therefore contrasts his "scientific" theory of revolution with the "spontaneous ideology" of the proletariat, which tends to be either highly romantic or merely reformist in nature. A plausible assumption underlies Marx's insistence that a professional thinker like himself has better insight into the remedy for the proletariat's condition; namely, members of the class generally lack the training and detachment for an objective appraisal of their situation. Thus Marx himself implies that the enlightenment and leadership of the proletariat must originate *outside* the class.

The missing explanation of how the proletariat first comprehends the necessity for revolution and then acts accordingly may be the most serious lacuna in Marxism. Left to its own devices the proletariat inclines toward accommodation with the ruling class. The propertyless workers tend to seek and to accept reforms from the capitalists, and this tendency undermines their initiation of radical, comprehensive changes in society. The point can be stated in more prosaic terms.

An impoverished and subjugated class naturally wishes to alleviate its plight. The question, though, is how much sacrifice reasonably can be anticipated of such a class when it decides to act. For instance, that an end to social division would benefit the proletariat as the lowest class in no way implies either (a) that the proletarians themselves will even comprehend the advantages that would accrue to them in a classless society or (b) that their conscious desire to construct such a society will be matched by a willingness to risk their meager possessions and even their lives in a revolution against the bourgeoisie. The history of Western Europe and North America during the past century suggests that the proletariat usually manages to settle its differences with the bourgeoisie without recourse to social upheaval. Improved wages, better living and working conditions, more access to educational and other opportunities, promises of additional reform have had the effect of deradicalizing the proletariat.

This brief digression has illustrated the implausibility of supposing that a commitment to revolution will originate within the proletariat itself. It must be emphasized, however, that Marx himself draws this conclusion. But if the propertyless workers require outside enlightenment and leadership in order to accomplish their mission, then the danger immediately arises that their political activity will degenerate into a simple seizure of power. An example may be welcome here.

As a practicing revolutionary who had to contend with the exigencies of his historical situation, Lenin was forced to act on the heretical principle that the proletariat's revolution should take place *before* the proletarians themselves became fully aware of its necessity and ultimate purpose. Consequently, the revolution of 1917 reflected the activity of a small group rather than the proletariat as a whole. The elitist character of this revolution accounts in part for the centralized, bureaucratic state that subsequently directed the nation's affairs. A skeptic might suspect that the Russian Revolution was just a political struggle, and the Soviet state's failure to show any sign of "withering away" lends credence to this suspicion. Rulers like Stalin often emerge as czars who lack only the title and aristocratic polish. That a political revolution does not have a truly democratic origin in fact increases the danger that its aftermath may perpetuate rather than terminate suppression of the many by the few.

Marx's theory about the transition from capitalism to a higher stage of civilization deserves acceptance only if it passes the usual test of accuracy, and it fails the test if proletarian politics move in either one of two directions: first, the proletariat's inclination to settle for internal reforms diverts it from a revolution against capitalism; second, the proletariat participates in a political revolution that fails to move beyond a mere seizure of power toward the transformation of society. The point here is not to argue that proletarian politics necessarily takes one of these two turns. It suffices to repeat that Marx adduces evidence against his own predictions about both the occurrence and the final outcome of a proletarian revolution. His analysis of capitalism enumerates the very forces that impede the enlightenment and consequent mobilization of the class. Further, the recent history of the West suggests that Marx underestimated the viability of capitalism, which has demonstrated its ability to accommodate the proletariat without capitulating to radical demands. In its lack of sympathy for radical politics the working class in contemporary America shows how far the accommodation has gone. Finally, the communist experience in the Eastern bloc indicates that Marx did not give proper emphasis to the Machiavellian factor in revolution. Many of the nations that currently proclaim a commitment to Marxism have not gone beyond dictatorial politics in the direction of a truly egalitarian society. The conclusion must be that both sociological and historical data tend to disconfirm Marx's forecast that the proletariat can engage in a successful revolt that will lead to the transformation of society.

This critique of Marx's utopianism has centered on the charge that his theory about the proletariat's revolution suffers from unrealistic and even romantic suppositions. Marx holds that the degradation and powerlessness of the proletariat fail to preclude its enlightenment and subsequent involvement in a revolution against the bourgeoisie; but he does not elaborate on how a suppressed class can be enlightened on the need for revolution so that it acts appropriately after its enlightenment. These lacunae in Marx's theory enhance the suspicion that his predictions about proletarian politics have little foundation in fact. The discussion of Marxism cannot end on this note, though. Chapter 4 considers the real source of Marx's utopianism: his theory of man.

4
Utopianism and Progress

Man's Role in History

Marxism draws no sharp distinction between the human and nonhuman determinants of history; instead, the theory emphasizes the way in which man interacts with the rest of reality in structuring and restructuring his civilization and, therefore, himself. For instance, one principle of Marxism states that a society's productive forces influence its overall character; hence the politics of an industrial nation should differ from those of an agrarian community. The point here is that the forces in question include both machinery and human labor power.

Marx's decision to count man among the forces that form and transform civilization can be construed as a reaction against two competing positions. The first overstates the importance of the human element, as in Caryle's thesis that great men make history. The second position errs in the opposite direction by underestimating the human factor, as in Calvin's doctrine of divine predestination. Marx tries to secure a place between such extremes. In opposition to the first he notes that a single individual seems almost impotent with respect to the other determinants of history; even the most powerful leader sometimes experiences the frustration of being unable to alter the course of events. Marx's rejection of the first position, however, hardly leads him to embrace the second. He does not reduce man to a passive victim of history but insists that man is a major historical force; hence each individual partially determines the content and direction of history, although obviously great differences in influence may exist.

Marx's views on man fall within his theory of history. Nonetheless, these views warrant separate consideration because of their importance in his explanation of progress, especially his forecast about the step from capitalism to a higher form of civilization. Since Marx regards social conflict and its culmination in revolution as essential for the advance of society, and since men play the key roles in the drama that surrounds revolution, Marx's account of man bears directly on his predictions about progress.

The Reciprocal Development of Needs and Powers

Marx's account of man centers on the idea that needs and powers (abilities) interact constantly so that they have a parallel development. Man's basic or biological needs originally impel him to work; hence labor originates as a response to the requirement for food and other essentials. But work does more than fulfill a given need. First, it enhances man's powers or his ability to gratify his desires. In some modern nations, for instance, agricultural technology has been so developed that starvation no longer threatens most of the population; such progress indicates an increase in man's powers. Second, work creates new needs in the process of satisfying older ones. Thus people quickly develop novel and often bizarre desires once their elementary needs have been gratified; the rich, for example, often have needs more unusual and extensive than those of the poor. In any case man's rudimentary needs inspire work that caters to them, and the new needs that arise from fulfillment of prior ones can be satisfied because man's powers grow at a comparable rate. This claim deserves scrutiny. The exercise of man's powers in response to his present needs reportedly has an amazing effect; namely, those powers increase in perfect proportion to the new needs that emerge from satisfaction of previous ones. The claim can be summarized as the thesis that needs and powers develop reciprocally.

The thesis that man's powers remain commensurate with his needs has strongly utopian connotations. It implies that human desire need not be frustrated in principle, for if man's needs never outstrip his powers he always has the ability to satisfy any drive he may develop. Marx's own statement of the thesis exhibits this utopianism. "Mankind always takes up only such problems as it can solve; since, looking at the matter more closely, we always will find that the problem itself arises only when the material conditions for its solution already exist or at least are in the process of formation."[1] This passage can be translated into the language of needs and powers by substituting these two words for "problem" and "solution," respectively. Thus man's ever-evolving needs define the "problems" to be solved, while his growing powers furnish him with the "solutions" to those problems. The passage can be explained further with reference to Marx's predictions about communism.

During the capitalist era man finally assumes an indisputably dominant position within nature, for under capitalism he first gains the economic power to satisfy his need for material security. Once man's biological needs receive reasonable gratification, however, higher needs begin to appear, the most important of which may be the universal desire for freedom. The point can be clarified by investigating the limits of freedom under capitalism. Freedom within this society seems confined to an elite whose members escape the economic coercion behind alienating labor. Of course, the capitalists may waste the opportunity for freedom by becoming bondsmen to their own greed, but they still retain the real possibility of freedom. The remainder of society, notably the proletarians, have only political liberty, but even this kind of freedom turns out to be spurious apart from economic freedom. For instance, the right to run for public office seems meaningless to a propertyless worker who must spend nearly all of his energy just to stay alive. The situation can be characterized as follows: capitalism undermines even the political (partial) freedom of the proletariat by denying the class economic and other social (full) freedom.

The limits to freedom under capitalism become increasingly obsolete and irrational as its economy gains efficiency through increased automation. If a society can guarantee each citizen a reasonably secure life, its division along economic lines amounts to the needless perpetuation of social conflict. That is, domination of the many by the few should cease once the problem of material scarcity has been solved. This theme now can be expressed with reference to the above quotation from Marx. Capitalism generates the wealth that gratifies man's need for economic security, and the gratification of this need engenders such higher needs as the universal desire for (full) freedom. This new need defines a problem to be solved—namely, the proletariat's emancipation from the bourgeoisie. At the same time, capitalism furnishes man with the power to solve the problem of universal liberation, for its economy equips him with enough wealth (especially the highly automated means of production) so that socially divided labor, the domination of one class by another, alienating work can be exterminated. In summary, capitalist affluence first creates the need for (full) freedom on a universal basis, and it enables mankind to satisfy the need through construction of a communist utopia.

The interaction between needs (problems) and powers (solutions) has been discussed on a very general level so far. The time has come to analyze more closely Marx's contention that powers keep pace with new needs. Again the topic will be discussed with reference to the proletarian revolution.

It seems plausible to suggest that the *universal* need for (full) freedom arises under capitalism. This society espouses democracy; hence capitalist ideology promotes the aspiration for freedom even within the lowest class. Further, that the wealth and corresponding power of the ruling class give them the opportunity to exhibit their freedom offers a striking example to those whose poverty denies them such a chance; the proletariat's envy of the bourgeoisie therefore may become tantamount to a desire for (full) freedom. Finally, capitalism offers impressive illustrations of how once-remote possibilities can be transformed into fact; in light of these accomplishments the proletariat's ambition for freedom may appear no more unrealistic than, say, the transition from hand mill to steam mill. Thus the economic miracle and the democratic commitment of capitalism supply an atmosphere in which the need for freedom may easily reach universal proportions.

The proletariat finds itself in servitude because of its poverty; consequently, its newly acquired need for (full) freedom originates as a desire to liberate itself from capitalist oppression. According to Marx, of course, the proletariat's emancipation begins with its seizure of power from the bourgeoisie. The question now arises about whether the proletariat, especially as described in Marxism, has the power to gratify its need for freedom. Perhaps the best way to attempt an answer here consists in breaking this question down into several rhetorical ones.

1. Can the proletariat counterbalance the liabilities of belonging to an impoverished and suppressed class as it participates in a political struggle? For instance, can the proletariat muster sufficient physical and mental energy for difficult political action after it spends long hours at manual labor? Can the proletariat's need for liberation offset its lack of education, scanty political experience, scarcity of all resources?

2. Can the proletariat find able leaders for its revolution, either by producing them within itself or by getting them from another

class? Can this propertyless class depend on those who seek to enlighten it on, and lead it in, a political battle? For instance, can the proletarians on the whole become shrewd enough to prevent their leaders from betraying the ultimate aims of the revolution against the bourgeoisie?

3. Finally, can the proletariat transform its seizure of power into a genuine social revolution? Can the proletariat withstand temptations for revenge, wealth, personal glory that threaten to reduce its (assumed) political success to just one more exchange of power? Will the lofty goal of a truly free society be traded off for short-range gains?

Satisfactory answers to these questions cannot be given yet. The chapters that follow lay the basis for pessimistic responses to most of them; at present, however, only the direction of the ensuing discussion can be indicated.

Marx's analysis of man, particularly with respect to the proletarian revolution, has at least one advantage over competing accounts about the end of social enslavement. Marx emphasizes that the "realm of freedom" will not be instituted so long as it remains a mere ideal in the minds of certain philosophers; he understands that this realm can be transported from the world of ideas and ideals into the real world only after freedom has become a *need* in those with the power to achieve it. His prediction of a proletarian revolution therefore rests on the premise that the propertyless workers will come to experience freedom as a pressing need instead of just a lofty ideal. But Marxism begins to falter in its explanation of how the proletariat acquires the power to gratify its need for freedom.

The Implausibility of Marx's Vision

The general difficulty with Marx's forecasts about communism can be expressed in this way. In his picture of social revolution

Marx portrays man as a being in whom needs and powers develop concurrently because a relation of reciprocal causation holds between them. Yet the picture lacks an essential feature; namely, its boundaries have not been demarcated. In less metaphorical language, Marx fails to indicate the limits of progress or the point at which man's powers can no longer match his needs. By claiming that man's powers always keep pace with his needs, Marx implies that no such point exists. The remainder of this study attempts to discredit Marx's utopianism by arguing that the limits of progress can be specified even at present. More specifically, it will be argued that the growth of man's powers has a restricted range even though his needs can expand indefinitely.

II
The
Antiutopian
Critique

I cannot bring a world quite round,
  Although I patch it as I can.

                    Wallace Stevens

5
Depth Psychology and Social Theory

The Search for a New Perspective

The analysis of Marx ended on a critical note: his account of man is unjustifiably optimistic because it affirms the perfect coordination of human needs and powers. Apparently, however, this criticism need not touch other aspects of Marxism, such as its insights into alienation, its distinction between merely political and true freedom, or its insistence on revolution as a vehicle of social progress. The omission of these and related topics from the preceding critique suggests that Marxism can be refashioned to avoid the charge of romanticism; namely, its conjecture about man's powers keeping pace with his needs could be dropped in favor of a more realistic appraisal.

Revision rather than discard of Marx's work appears advantageous at first glance because this approach would preserve his contributions to the study of history, sociology, political theory, and other fields; it seems rash to reject all of Marxism merely because part of it cannot withstand criticism. Nonetheless, no attempt to revise Marxism will be made here. Two considerations recommend this decision.

First, the highly systematic nature of Marxism makes the job of revamping it almost forbidding. Marx's views on man do not represent an independent or detachable item in his system; on the contrary, his views have been integrated so thoroughly into the system that any treatment of them in isolation becomes artificial. No sharp boundaries separate Marx's reflections on history from his sociology, or his teaching on man from his doctrine of revolution. Marxism resists by design any effort to break it down into neatly divided, subordinate disciplines; hence to invest Marxism with a new account of man presents difficulties whose solution would require at least another book.

The second reason for avoiding a revision of Marxism stems from the main intent of this book, which is to study two competing accounts of unhappiness. The utopian position has been illustrated with orthodox Marxism. If a reconstructed Marxism now were introduced to represent the antiutopian alternative, the issue of unhappiness might be lost among the details of Marxism. In the interest of sharpening the contrast between utopian and antiutopian approaches to this issue, it seems advisable to disqualify every Marxist theory as an example of the antiutopian. Freudianism admirably fits this requirement. It differs from Marxism on the key point because Freudian theory offers an antiutopian analysis of unhappiness. Freud's approach to the issue also differs from that of Marx; Freud's heavy reliance data from psychotherapy illustrates the difference. Finally, that Freud's vocabulary contains virtually none of Marx's jargon lends additional emphasis to their disagreement on the substantive matter.

The study of Freudian theory will be patterned after the analysis of Marxism. This chapter will trace the lines of inquiry, which then can be pursued in the next two chapters. The study will begin with a tentative characterization of depth psychology.

The Inadequacy of Behaviorism

Depth psychology can be characterized provisionally as the alternative to a behavioristic study of the self. Of course, this characterization cannot aid the discussion until the notion of behaviorism has been clarified. In common with so many other nouns that designate schools of thought, the word *behaviorism* permits multiple and perhaps even conflicting readings. The term may be restricted in application, for instance, so that it covers only the kind of psychology that self-proclaimed behaviorists certify. On a broader and less arbitrary interpretation, any brand of psychology may qualify as behavioristic as long as it adheres to the principle that conclusions about the self must be founded exclusively on the data of publicly observable behavior. Neither of these interpretations will be adopted here. The first seems far too capricious and narrow: the second has little descriptive value because it makes virtually every theory of the self behavioristic in at least a minimal sense.

Behaviorism is understood here as the theory that affirms that the self can be adequately explained without attributing to it such unobservable components as an unconsciousness or a soul. The theory acknowledges that the self usually shares certain features and abilities with other members of the race (for instance, two lungs and the capacity to think abstractly); it also allows that every person has a genetic endowment that helps to individuate him within the species. Although these two factors have a place in the explanatory scheme of behaviorism they fail to receive the same attention as the environment. Behaviorism analyzes the self chiefly in terms of its responses to such external stimuli as parental training, education, and other kinds of conditioning. This emphasis reflects the conviction that different actions of the self can be correlated in principle with specific external stimuli.

Drawing such correlations provides a causal explanation of behavior. A simple example may be instructive. A child who says "red" whenever his parent holds a red toy before him while asking

"What color is it?" responds to two stimuli—the color of the toy and his parent's verbal cue. These stimuli may be designated *variables* because their presence and absence correspond with different behavior; the child presumably utters the word *red* only in response to the appropriate stimuli. The self's unique genetic inheritance and its generically human traits can be called *constants* because they furnish a relatively stable background against which external stimuli change; hence the child himself seems to remain basically the same person throughout the appearance and disappearance of various external stimuli. The variable-constant distinction now can be employed to clarify behavioristic explanation; namely, such an explanation specifies the variables whose presence usually elicits a particular response from the self. In this light behaviorism appears as an attempt to adopt a Pavlovian model of causality in explaining the self's activity: stimuli from the environment constitute the "causes" behind certain modes of behavior, which, in turn, count as the "effects" or conditioned responses of these stimuli.[1]

In some respects behaviorism offers an appealing model of the self. If behavior could be explained adequately and primarily in terms of external stimuli (causes) and conditioned responses (effects), then enumeration of these stimuli would support predictions about behavior. Such predictions could serve as the basis for controlling behavior; namely, the self would be exposed only to those stimuli that elicited desired—and presumably desirable—responses. Behaviorism apparently opens the door to the discovery of techniques that will permit man to determine his actions; then, on the provision that this human engineering takes a positive turn, such evils as war would be eradicated through the manipulation of external stimuli.

A closer inspection of behaviorism, however, discloses flaws that distract from its initially attractive countenance. It is implausible to suggest that man, the most complex of the organisms, can be studied on the model of a computer whose output (conditioned responses) correlates neatly with its input (external stimuli). Further, the proposal to explicate behavior by matching external stimuli with responses deserves acceptance solely on the condition that meaningful correlations can be drawn in practice. An earlier example illustrates the point.

Assume that the child who usually says *red* in response to the question about the color of a red toy sometimes gives an intentionally incorrect answer, such as *green*. This reply might be attributed to the child's impatience or irritation over the lesson, and his uttering of the word *green* can be construed as a response to the prolonged repetition of the same external stimuli (namely, presentation of a red toy and the question "What color is it?"). Suppose, in addition, that the child's deliberately wrong answers follow no obvious pattern. At times he completes the lesson without an error, at other times he makes an intentional mistake at the very beginning, and so forth. An account of his behavior in terms of external stimuli now becomes more involved. The range of these stimuli must be extended to encompass such additional factors as the noises that kept the child from getting enough sleep before his lesson, or the suggestion of a mischievous friend that he feign ignorance about the toy's color. If no correlation between these external stimuli and the response *green* can be discovered, still other factors must be introduced into the explanation of his deliberate mistakes. Clearly, this process of addition might have to be continued indefinitely. At some point, however, so many external stimuli would be needed to explain the child's simple act of deceit that the explanation itself would become absurdly complicated and therefore practically useless.

The child's pretended ignorance resists a thoroughly behavioristic explanation because of its spontaneous character. As a matter of common experience a human being sometimes does not seem to react at all to external stimuli; he may behave as if his circumstances and previous training had no influence whatsoever on him. An act of courage by a former coward illustrates the point. The relative independence of man's behavior from his environment and conditioning makes him the most unpredictable of the animals. But if a person can act quite differently in almost the same conditions, then virtually identical stimuli that impinge on essentially the same individual may fail to produce corresponding similar responses. This point should be a source of embarrassment to behaviorism because it implies the inadequacy of explaining man's activity principally as responses conditioned by external stimuli.[2]

Naturally this critique of behaviorism cannot be regarded as support for any one brand of depth psychology, including Freudianism, but it offers the initial justification for looking to non-behavioristic psychology in the search for a satisfactory account of the self. It should be expected that such an account will forsake the attempt to explain behavior primarily in terms of observable stimuli from the environment conditioning responses in the self. Instead, depth psychology counts unobservable components and functions in the self (for example, the unconsciousness and the process of repression) among the causes of behavior. To admit the unobservable nature of such components and functions may arouse the suspicion that they do not exist at all. Perhaps the only way to counter this objection consists in recalling the inadequacy of behaviorism, which scrupulously avoids positing unobservable causes. For just this reason a behavioristic explanation emphasizes the causal role of *external*—namely, publicly observable—stimuli. If behaviorism cannot provide a satisfactory account of man, its replacement must be a theory that acknowledges the contribution of unobservable or merely inferred causes to behavior. For the sake of both economy and prudence the number of unobservable causes should be kept at a minimum, but the point still remains that an adequate theory of the self cannot ignore these causes.

Freudianism and Social Theory

One aim of this chapter has been to offer a preliminary description of depth (nonbehavioristic) psychology; a second aim has been to present a partial justification for such a psychology. Completion of these tasks requires that the discussion move to a less general level by considering a case in point, Freudianism. The coming discussion also must initiate the dialog between Freud and Marx. Some preparations for this dialog already have been made. The preceding chapters indicated how Marx's social theory contains a distinct account of man; so this account eventually can be related to its Freudian counterpart on the issue of unhappiness. First, however, Freud's social theory must be located within his psychology, for, at least initially, Freud appears to speak about man as an isolated patient of psychotherapy while Marx talks about him as an essentially social animal. Chapter 6 attempts to show that Freud's depth psychology includes a sophisticated social theory. Once the details of the theory have been elaborated, the stage should be set for the contrast between Marxism and Freudianism as representatives of the utopian and the antiutopian positions on unhappiness.

6
Freud and
the Conservatism of
the Instincts

Psychoanalysis as Theory and Therapy

Near the end of the highly speculative work, *Civilization and Its Discontents*, Freud considers a dilemma that arises at the center of psychoanalysis. The practicing analyst must assume that society at large is normal; otherwise he could not justify any attempt to reconcile his neurotic or somehow abnormal patient with the often harsh demands of the environment. The practice of psychoanalysis proceeds under the supposition that the community as a whole furnishes a standard of normalcy against which individual members can be compared in diagnosing mental illness. Thus the term *neurotic* indicates a person who needs treatment because he differs in some noteworthy way from the rest of the community. In summary, the presumption that society should count as psychologically normal generates one horn of Freud's dilemma.

Another horn of the dilemma can be explained with reference to a key tenet in psychoanalysis, the biogenetic law. This law is, roughly, that the individual's psychological development recapitulates, over a relatively short period of time, the cultural evolution of the species; conversely, the history of civilization reflects the formation of the human personality. If the biogenetic law is true, though, and if psychological development in some individuals runs amiss and produces neurotics, then presumably an entire society also can be psychologically defective; hence the truth of the biogenetic law would seem to imply the possibility that civilization as such might become infected with mental illness.[1] In such circumstances the practice of psychoanalysis may be both futile and reprehensible. Since the patient's acclimation to his (social) environment is a primary aim of such analysis, its success within a neurotic culture ironically causes or reinforces rather than cures or relieves mental illness; the intended psychotherapy makes the patient just as sick as everyone else.

So the possibility that society should not count as psychologically normal generates the second horn of Freud's dilemma. That is, the practice of psychoanalysis must rest on the assumption that society as a whole enjoys psychological health, for society provides the norm against which the individual's condition can be evaluated. However, theoretical principles such as the biogenetic law, which suggests the possibility of communal neurosis, also belong to psychoanalysis, and a sick civilization undermines psychotherapy by denying the analyst a standard against which he can judge his patients' mental health.

Freud's dilemma illustrates the tension that often exists between theory and practice. In psychoanalysis neither theory nor practice (therapy) has a clear claim to primacy. Theoretical principles like the biogenetic law are not just expendable dogmas; Freud goes so far as to base the authenticity of his program for psychotherapy on the truth of psychoanalytic theory. Conversely, practical psychoanalysis cannot be understood as a mere application of the theory; at many points Freud's theory directly reflects his experience in the clinic. The way Freud eases the tension between the two faces of psychoanalysis will be considered later. At present, the important point concerns the theory-therapy distinction itself, because this distinction helps to explain how Freud's depth psychology can serve as his social theory. The matter can be clarified by returning to the previously mentioned passages from *Civilization and Its Discontents*.

After posing the question of whether mental illness can beset a whole culture, Freud mentions a problem in offering a straightforward answer; namely, no criterion seems available to diagnose a communal neurosis. For example, if one society S were condemned as neurotic on the grounds that it compared unfavorably with a presumably sane society S', the question still would remain whether S' should serve as the norm for sanity, for S' might also be sick. Additional comparisons involving S' and S'', then S'' and S''', and so on, obviously would not diminish the difficulty; such comparisons would start a vicious, infinite regress in which no final comparison ever could be reached. Distinction between normalcy and neurosis on the level of whole societies appears problematical at best. Freud therefore talks about the "pathology of cultural communities" as a project rather than an accomplishment of psychoanalysis. Finally, he warns that such psychoanalytic conceptions as sanity and normalcy should be applied to entire societies only with caution. Since these notions pertain originally to individuals, their analogical extension to societies may be more misleading than enlightening.

The main purpose of the preceding discussion has been to show one side of Freud's complicated attitude toward social theory. Sometimes when he assumes the stance of a psychotherapist Freud speaks as if his remarks about civilization in general should be regarded as an appendage to a solid body of psychotherapeutic technique; hence he occasionally displays the impatience of a busy physician whose concern for his patients leaves little time for speculation about social theory. But the antitheoretical slant in some of Freud's writings cannot be allowed to obscure the idea that psychoanalysis not only permits but also encourages interpretation as speculative social theory. This claim can be expressed in an even stronger fashion. Freudian psychotherapy is designed to forge a compromise between the individual's incessant demands for happiness and society's persistent refusal to fully honor those demands. Psychoanalytic theory reflects this aim with the principle that an enduring but usually well-controlled conflict mars the relationship between the individual and his social environment. The conflict allegedly does not confine itself to a few societies or to certain periods of history. Unlike Marx, for example, Freud never believed that the demise of capitalism would move man any closer to utopia. Freud views the antagonism between the individual and society as implacable, a pessimistic view that can be traced to his theory of instincts. According to the theory, the repression of man's basic desires for happiness is both the precondition for survival *and* the originating, sustaining force of civilization. These points will be discussed in greater detail below.

Is the Theory of Instincts a Freudian Myth?

The suggestion that Freud's theory of instincts can contribute to an understanding of civilization may invite ridicule, especially since Freud himself admits that the instincts are mythical entities.[2] He says that the instincts remain inaccessible to direct inspection; they can be studied only through their manifestations or effects in (overt) behavior. Nevertheless, Freud never abandons the theory but works continuously on its refinement. In order to appreciate how his seemingly pejorative characterization of the instincts fails to conflict with his defense of their importance, it will be helpful to consider again the theory-therapy distinction within psychoanalysis.

Freud's formulation of a theory about the instincts represents, first, an effort to systematize the data he and other experts gathered from extensive clinical studies on mental disorder; hence the theory grew out of actual experiences with psychotherapy. The point can be explained more adequately with an example.

In his classical work on psychotherapy, *The Interpretation of*

Dreams, Freud introduces a "topographical" analysis of the psyche. [He cautions, however, that the topography should be distinguished sharply from an ordinary map; since the psyche has no spatial dimensions it cannot be mapped in a literal sense.] Freud's demarcation of psychic areas is not to be taken in a literal sense and therefore ought to be interpreted only as an explanatory device. In any case, the topographical analysis divides the psyche into three distinct regions: (U) the unconscious; (P) the preconscious; (C) the conscious. The primary difference between (U) and (P) concerns the way their respective contents (for instance, a memory) can cross the boundary that separates the two regions from (C). Specifically, the contents of (P) can be made conscious by such ordinary means as voluntary recall, while those of (U) can be brought to consciousness only through an extraordinary device such as psychoanalysis. That is, (P) contains thoughts and feelings that may have been temporarily forgotten or have not yet acquired sufficient intensity for passing through the threshold to consciousness, but (U) contains thoughts and desires that are held under constant pressure, which prevents their emergence from the unconscious depths of the psyche into consciousness. The point can be summarized by saying that (U) alone contains *repressed* psychic contents. The initial task of the psychotherapist involves release of the force behind the repression so that the patient then can become aware of previously unconscious thoughts and desires. The cure occurs when the patient finally accepts that these repressed items constitute infantile, unrealistic wishes for perfect happiness, a point that warrants additional clarification.

According to Freud, even the most mature adult cannot escape a residual infantile ambition for unconditional pleasure; in terms of the topography no one can empty his unconsciousness of repressed wishes from early life. A neurotic, however, may be unable to accept that these wishes can be neither realistically fulfilled nor completely abandoned; so he attempts to fulfill them in a roundabout way (for instance, through extended daydreaming). In order to cure such a person the psychoanalyst must elicit from him an act of resignation; the neurotic must be brought to renounce his disguised efforts at satisfying his infantile ambitions for happiness. The neurosis begins to end with the patient's resolution that he will endure the irremediable conflict between the demands of his unconscious (repressed) life and the unpleasant reality of his conscious life.

The topography now can be related to the theory of instincts. Freud locates the instincts in the unconscious, and he characterizes infantile wishes for perfect happiness as instinctual. The characterization emphasizes at least three features of these wishes. First, they remain inaccessible to ordinary investigation; they can be studied only with such special psychoanalytic tools as the interpretation of dreams. Second, these wishes help to unify the species in the sense that human beings, like other animals, share with one another certain drives. Third, the suppressed wishes influence all behavior; they furnish the unconscious foundation that supports conscious or higher activity, such as art. The main point here, however, is that Freud's use of such theoretical constructs as the topography or notion of an instinct cannot be dismissed as idle speculation; these constructs generally have a solid basis in the practice of psychoanalysis. Reference to one problem in psychotherapy provides an illustration.

Freud and his fellow psychotherapists often encountered strong resistance when they tried to confront a patient with a traumatic event of the past. The patient's defensiveness cannot be explained away as embarrassment over an ordinary lapse in memory; all of the psychotherapist's attempts to restore the presumably forgotten event to the patient's consciousness induce only more antagonism. On the basis of such clinical evidence Freud maintains that a trauma is not just lost in the patient's memory; it is actively if unconsciously suppressed. The distinction between the preconscious and the unconscious explains the difference in question; namely, a merely forgotten event lies within the region of the preconscious, while a suppressed trauma falls within the area of the unconscious. Thus such notions as (U) and (P) provide a theoretical apparatus for explaining such clinically documented facts as the patient's resistance to psychotherapy.

To claim that Freud's first or (U)-(P)-(C) topography has roots in psychotherapeutic fact is not to imply that each item in his theory reflects an experience in the clinic. Since the theory of instincts sometimes seems quite abstract and technical, however, its connection with psychoanalytic practice should be noted; so the sections that will follow continue to indicate how elements in the theory relate to the data of psychotherapy.

Work with patients provides Freud with some but certainly not all of the data he consults in building the theory of instincts; he also appeals to obvious facts about man's condition. In a letter to Einstein on the perennial threat of war, for instance, Freud refers to his later theory of instincts, in which man's drives fall into two primary groups: the erotic or Life instincts and the destructive (aggressive) or Death instincts. Since war constitutes one kind of aggressive behavior, Freud suggests that his theory may throw light on the topic. Significantly, however, he remarks that his division of instincts into erotic and destructive categories corresponds roughly to the "universally familiar" polarity of love and hate; in brief, he insists that his theory about the instincts has its basis in common sense. Freud goes on to say that all behavior shows the confluence of the two primary instincts, and he offers ordinary examples in defense of the thesis. Thus preservation of the species relies on the erotic instincts for the procreation of new generations; it also receives help from the destructive instincts in the mastery of nature. The element of mystery in Freud's theory about the instincts tends to disappear as he relates the theory to familiar behavior.[3]

As noted earlier, Freud's theory of instincts invites scepticism because it deals with admittedly mythical entities. With less pejorative language and ample justification, Freud might have called the instincts *inferred* as against *directly observed* components of the self. This change in terminology would have capped the theory with a halo of scientific respectability, since even physics, a highly reputable discipline, makes reference to merely inferred entities. At any rate, Freud does not use the theory in order to obscure the facts of mental pathology and everyday life; instead, he relies on it as an explanatory construct in which data from many sources can be organized and explained. This use of the theory aims at making the facts more rather than less intelligible. Perhaps Freud's own attitude toward the theory of instincts comes across best in a passage from *Civilization and Its Discontents*. In introducing the sixth section of the book Freud confesses that his comments on the effects of the Life and Death instincts seem obviously and even trivially true. He therefore apologizes because the phenomena he explains with a theory about the instincts may require no explanation at all.

The formal defense of Freud's theory of instincts ends here, but the defense will continue informally in the argument for the theory as an excellent perspective from which to view the issue of unhappiness.

The Theory of Instincts in Four Explanatory Models

At least two traits in Freud's theory of instincts frustrate his ambition to avoid obfuscation. First, he often explains the theory with figures of speech. In presenting the first topography, for example, he sometimes writes as if the psyche contained spatially distinct compartments that correspond to specific psychological activities. The use of tropes raises problems of clarity, especially since metaphor and analogy frequently allow more than one interpretation. It should not be surprising, then, that parts of Freud's theory invite conflicting readings. Second, he subjects the theory to almost constant revision; yet no change entails a total rejection of an earlier version. The theory of instincts grows to maturity through the extension and refinement of basic insights, and the final formulation of the theory shows traces of each earlier version. In light of these considerations it is convenient to approach the theory in the following way. First, the theory is examined with reference to four explanatory models Freud uses; although the models remain distinct, elements from one usually can be found in the others. Second, a short developmental sketch of the theory is given. Third, the ramifications of the theory are discussed.

One explanatory model, the topography, already has received attention, but its treatment in the last section needs to be supplemented, mainly because Freud presents two topographies. The first divides the psyche or self into the now-familiar regions of (U) unconsciousness, (P) preconsciousness, and (C) consciousness. The second topography also offers a tripartite division of the self, but the new distinctions among id, ego, and superego do not correspond neatly to those of the first topography. Incidentally, the Latin terms do not originate in Freud; he uses substantives of ordinary German pronouns: *das Es* (the it), *das Ich* (the I), and *das Überich* (the super-I). The point deserves mention because the Latinized translations have technical connotations that Freud's own choices lack. In any case the constituents of the second topography can be characterized provisionally as follows. The id represents the instinctual or nonrational agency in the self; it promotes the self's continuous search after pleasure. The ego serves as the agency that gives rational direction to the search; the ego tries to establish harmony between the ambitions of the instincts and reality. The superego acts as society's envoy in the self; it tries to elicit socially acceptable behavior from the self. These descriptions can be elaborated by considering several connections between the two topographies. First, however, it is necessary to expand the previous analysis of the first topography.

The earlier exposition ignored one of its constituents, the *censor*, which guards the border that separates (U) from (P) and (C). The censor's presence along this boundary reflects, on a theoretical level, the fact of psychoanalytic practice that the journey from (U) to (C) encounters far more resistance than a movement from

(P) to (C). Only with aid from such a special vehicle as psychoanalysis can a once-unconscious desire or thought enter consciousness; but an ordinary attempt at remembering can transport a preconscious idea or feeling into (C). Concisely, the censor represses the contents of (U) so that they cannot escape into (P) and (C). These contents include those infantile wishes for absolute happiness that even the mature person cannot renounce completely; so the censor protects the conscious self as best it can from the imposition of troublesome infantile desires. The censor also accounts for the patient's resistance to the probings of the psychoanalyst, who aims at making the patient's unconscious life accessible to his consciousness.

After introducing the notion of the censor, Freud cautions that it should not be taken ``. . . as a stern little manikin or a spirit who lives in a little chamber of the brain and there discharges the duties of his office.''[4] His very use of the term, though, encourages such an anthropocentric interpretation—an interpretation that carries over to the superego, which in the second topography assumes some of the roles the censor plays in the first topography. The superego also has a rough counterpart in common sense; namely, in some respects it resembles conscience. The multiple functions of the superego require discussion.

Just as the censor controls unconscious, infantile wishes by preventing them from overwhelming the conscious self, so the superego disciplines the id's drives by subordinating them to the ego's dictates. In performing its duty the censor protects consciousness from unrealistic wishes for pleasure; to the extent that the censor succeeds, the conscious self can entertain perceptions of the external world or thoughts about its course of action. These perceptions and thoughts obviously contribute to the difficult business of living far more than do infantile dreams about perfect happiness. The superego performs a comparable service for the ego as the ego tries to secure a working relationship between the self and the environment. The superego prevents the self from being dominated by the ultimately self-destructive drives of the id; hence the superego enables the ego to bring the self into a relatively harmonious relationship with its physical and social surroundings. That the id's drives deserve the word *self-destructive* can be shown through a simple example.

Since hungry infants lack the ability to discriminate between helpful and harmful substances, they cannot be left to their own devices. An infant's nearly constant urge to eat will result in its own death unless parents or their surrogates control satisfaction of the urge; only through such control can the infant's drive to eat work for rather than against its survival. Although Freud does not count the drive to eat among the primary instincts, this example can be used to illustrate the self-annihilating bent of the Life and Death (that is, the primary) instincts. All instincts inhabit the id, which Freud describes as timeless. His characterization implies that the self's drives never vary in essence from birth to death; only their manifestations in (overt) behavior change in the process of maturation. During the course of normal psychological develop-ment, however, the instincts become progressively controlled so that they no longer pose an immediate threat to life. Parental or other external authority first provides the required control over the instincts, but eventually the individual himself takes on the main burden of such control through self-discipline. In fact, effective self-control usually counts as the badge of adulthood. These points now can be transcribed into the jargon of the second topography.

At birth the id reigns in the self. It strives for full and immediate satisfaction of all the drives that compose it, but, as the example of the infant suggests, the undisciplined fulfillment of these drives ironically causes death. The id's unsupervised regulation of the self amounts to unwitting self-destruction, hence the need for *exter-nal* control (usually in the form of parental authority) over the self during the periods of infancy, childhood, and even adolescence. Gradually, however, the control becomes internalized as the self comes to recognize that the complete gratification of its drives makes life itself impossible. In slightly different language, the maturing self begins to comprehend the irrationality of the id's demands for perfect pleasure, demands that call, in effect, for self-destruction precisely because they remain blind to the threats that arise from the environment. In the infant, for example, the urge to eat can cause death because it draws no distinction between nutritious and poisonous objects.

Formation of the ego coincides with the self's gradual recognition that an uninhibited id threatens survival. Thus the ego represents the topographical agency that develops through interaction of the self with its physical and social surroundings. Once it has been sufficiently formed, the ego regulates commerce between the self and the external world; hence the mature ego runs the business of survival. But the ego need not restrain the id by itself; the superego performs most of that service. Freud describes the superego as "internalized" or "introjected" authority, because it takes over from parents and others the task of controlling the self's drives. That is, the superego originates with the child's imitation of its parents: "When we were children, we knew these higher beings, we admired them, and we feared them; and later we took them into ourselves."[5]

At first the superego exerts a relatively uncomplicated, yet crucial, kind of control over the id; namely, it prevents the id's urges from destroying the self. The superego's disciplinary influence over the id later assumes a moral or an ethical dimension so that the superego acts as the individual's conscience. The accretion of roles for the superego parallels the emergence of new responsibilities for the self. Since the superego matures along with the self in which it resides, it eventually comprises not only the introjected commands of parents but also the internalized customs, mores, expectations of society as a whole. In the end the superego must play the roles of protective parent, religious conscience, and idealized self. The last role deserves further consideration.

One cliché about adulthood states that the mature person should "live up to" his responsibilities. The phrase in quotation implies that a discrepancy may exist between behavior and obligations; then an adult probably will receive criticism from two sources. First, society probably will express its disapproval in some way; second, the individual may censure himself. Freud's later topography accounts for the second source. In forming the superego, the self introjects more than those explicitly decreed moral laws that make up the individual's conscience; the self also internalizes those often-unspoken but declared expectations against which the community judges its members. Thus, heavy drinking may not be condemned as sinful, but such behavior probably will be discouraged with a less severe expression of public disapproval. In any case the superego acts as the envoy through which society conveys to the self both explicit and implicit expectations. Since the self's interaction with the social environment occurs through the ego, the superego furnishes the ego with a standard or an ideal; the superego shows the ego how society expects the self to behave.

This exposition of the two topographies will facilitate the examination of Freud's other explanatory models. In summary, both topographies account for (overt) behavior with reference to regions and agencies in the self. The first topography, for instance, explains a patient's resistance to recalling a trauma with the notion of a censor who stands guard along the border that separates (U) from (P) and (C). The second topography clarifies the phenomenon of self-discipline and self-rebuke with the idea of internalized authority. Finally, Freud warns that the two topographies derive whatever validity they may have from their usefulness as explanatory devices; in no circumstances should they be construed as literal pictures of the self.

A second explanatory model through which Freud presents the theory of instincts may be labeled *mechanistic* because it treats the self as an elaborate machine or robot.[6] In constructing this model Freud borrows jargon from such mechanistically oriented disciplines as classical (Newtonian) physics, then current neurophysiology, electronics, and even hydraulics. For example, "cathexis" or the self's "investment" of some quantity of psychological "energy" in a desired object represents a key notion in the mechanistic model. Neurosis becomes a "detour" or, alternately, a "short circuit" along the "path" that connects instinctual wishes with their gratification. The detour leads directly to hallucination or some other form of substitute satisfaction for these wishes. Similarly, hysteria results from an "overload" of excitation in the self.

These mechanistically inclined explanations of behavior indicate Freud's wish to mold psychoanalysis in the image of reputable science; hence he sometimes proclaims his intention to make psychoanalysis into a "scientific psychology" or a "mathematical, quantitative science." Unfortunately, however, his project generates considerable confusion without winning many converts among the skeptics. The confusion arises because in fitting the mechanistic model to the psychoanalytic facts Freud often works at three or more terminological levels, and the exact way in which these levels interconnect remains a mystery. Freud's linguistic mixture usually contains ingredients from three sources—psychology, neurology, and physics. Thus such words as *wish* and *gratification*, which belong to psychology, mingle with terms from neurology such as *neuron* and *discharge*. This linguistic alliance then joins forces with jargon from physics, such as *particle* and *inertia*. Consequently, it remains unclear whether Freud believes that such psychological processes as wishing reduce without remainder to such physiological events as a chemical reaction in the central nervous system, or whether he thinks that psychological and physiological occurrences just parallel each other. The resolution of this difficulty in interpretation far exceeds the ambitions of the present discussion. It is sufficient here to indicate the kind of problem that results from Freud's mechanistic explanations of the self.[7]

Additional clarification of Freud's second explanatory construct concerns three notions: the pleasure, reality, and constancy principles. These principles can be clarified with reference to the two topographies.

The undisciplined id operates according to the pleasure principle. This conclusion follows from two considerations: first, the id represents the part of the self that strives for full and immediate gratification of instinctual desires; second, fulfillment of these desires brings pleasure. As noted earlier, however, the unregulated pursuit of pleasure leads directly to death. Since the self must contend with various threats and demands that arise from both the physical and the social environment, it cannot immediately and completely satisfy all of its urges and at the same time survive. The self must renounce some pleasure in order to live. Thus domination of the pleasure principle in the id cannot extend to the entire self; the reality principle must govern there in the interest of life.

It would be misleading to present the pleasure and reality principles as standing in direct opposition to each other. Even under the regulation of the reality principle the self tries to satisfy its drives. By following that principle, however, the search for pleasure ends with only the partial and delayed gratification of the instincts, for, again, their complete and instantaneous fulfillment ensures death alone. Under the direction of the reality principle the self adopts a policy of calculated hedonism; it attempts to work out a compromise between pleasure and survival. In this light the reality principle appears as the rationally amended version of the pure pleasure principle. The same point can be expressed in the language of the second topography.

Although the ego represents the topographical agency that promotes rational control over behavior, it retains continuity with the id—the agency that pushes for irrational (purely instinctual) regulation of the self. Specifically, formation of the ego results from the unavoidable confrontation between the id's relentless drive for absolute happiness and the exigencies of life in the real world. If this confrontation does not produce the ego—the agency that conducts the search for pleasure in a rational and restrained fashion —then the id will continue to govern the self under the pure pleasure principle until this course of action leads to death. If confrontation between the id and reality produces a sufficiently strong ego, however, then the self's quest for pleasure can proceed in accord with the reality principle, under which death ceases to be the exorbitant price the self must pay for its pleasure. In summary, the reality principle reigns in the ego, which strives for the disciplined and therefore realistic satisfaction of the instincts; the pure pleasure principle rules in the id, whose undisciplined pursuit of pleasure can end only in self-destruction.

The pleasure-reality distinction is not confined to Freud's mechanistic model of the self; the two principles have a place in other explanatory constructs. One distinguishing feature of the mechanistic model, though, is its identification of the pleasure principle with the *constancy*, or *stability*, principle, which comes to psychoanalysis as an offspring of the principle of inertia in classical physics. The constancy principle states that the self resists any (quantitative) rise in its level of tension; hence the self seeks to maintain its equilibrium with an "inertial" resistance against forces that threaten to disrupt its "homeostatic balance." Less technically, constancy consists in achieving and preserving a state of relaxation. Any (quantitative) increase in excitement constitutes pain or at least the absence of pleasure; every decrease in excitation brings pleasure. Following this line of thought, orgasm gives great pleasure because it sharply reduces sexual tension.

Perhaps the most serious objection against Freud's mechanistic model concerns the identification of pleasure with homeostasis. This equation rests on the supposition that pleasure can be treated in purely quantitative terms. In accord with the constancy principle, any decrease in the quantity of tension generates pleasure, and the amount of produced pleasure varies directly with the amount of reduced tension. This analysis of pleasure may be quite convincing in such examples as orgasm, but it apparently must be strained in order to cover, say, the kind of enjoyment that accompanies contemplation of an artistic masterpiece. Thus Freud's mechanistic account of pleasure may not discriminate sufficiently among types of pleasure. Although in Chapter 7 Freud is defended against such a criticism, the point remains that his analysis of *every* pleasure as reduced tension seems implausible.

Freud never abandons the thesis that pleasure consists in the (quantitative) reduction of tension, but in the later works he moves toward the position that at least one kind of pleasure does not fit the mechanistic explanation. The question of how he tries to resolve this apparent inconsistency cannot be answered yet; two remarks must suffice here. First, his suggestion that some pleasure may not involve a drop in the level of tension amounts to the concession that psychoanalysis cannot become a purely mathematical or quantitative psychology. Second, the variety and complexity of psychoanalytic data discourages merely quantitative analysis. For instance, the distinction between normal and abnormal conduct presumably must be drawn along qualitative lines; it therefore seems that correspondingly different explanations must be given for the kind of pleasure a neurotic derives from hallucination and the kind a normal person gains from an ordinary experience. A final judgment on Freud's mechanistic model cannot be given, however, until his other explanatory constructs have been studied.

Freud's third explanatory construct may be the most familiar, for it has become the keystone of popular psychoanalysis. It is called the *genetic* model, and its basic notions include such principles as the previously discussed biogenetic law and such concepts as regression and fixation. The genetic explanation concentrates on the influence that the past exercises on the development of both the individual and the species. Details of this explanation again can be given with reference to the two topographies.

Earlier discussions have alluded to two salient features of the id—its atemporal and impersonal character. To call the id atemporal or ahistorical is to emphasize that it never varies, since change presupposes time. But if the id undergoes no alteration, then each individual retains the same fundamental urges from birth to death. Thus the atemporal id represents the permanent instinctual core in every human being. To label the id impersonal is to suggest that it serves as an unconscious force that unites all men into a single species, despite those obvious differences in personality that distinguish them from one another. These related aspects of the id account for the preoccupation with the past that characterizes Freudian psychoanalysis. The way psychoanalytic theory justifies, and psychoanalytic practice applies, this preoccupation must be considered.

During the earliest periods of life the id enjoys a monarchical position in the self. Eventually, however, the id must defend its authority against the other two topographical agencies. The ensuing conflict arises because reality will not tolerate the survival of an organism under the exclusive guidance of the id; life under the pure pleasure principle leads directly to death. Thus in the interests of survival the ego and the superego try to erode and usurp the id's power by bringing the self's drive for pleasure under the reality principle. Details of the topographical war look like this. The ego and the id engage in what non-Freudians might call the battle between reason and the passions. The outcome of their struggle decides whether the self's pursuit of pleasure will be tempered with the rational control necessary for survival. Although reason frequently seems ineffectual against the sheer persistence of the passions, in quelling the id the ego obtains aid from the superego, whose primary function consists in directing instinctual energy away from self-destructive pleasure toward such socially useful activity as work. Thus, by disciplining the id the superego promotes both individual and communal survival. The superego's functions now must be related to the self's past.

The id's drive for unconditional pleasure never abates because the id's constitution varies not at all; hence the adult and the infant share basic urges. The many differences between them at the level of (overt) behavior stems from the respective controls under which these urges operate. The normal adult, who has a relatively well-developed ego and superego, usually can constrain his instincts without outside assistance. The infant, conversely, depends almost exclusively on his parents or their surrogates to control its id. The point of present interest is that the adult's system of internal control is the more effective. A trivial illustration is that adults rarely tolerate in themselves the same boorish behavior they praise as cute in their children; similarly, the indiscretions of infants and other inno-cents become matters of embarrassment and even shame when committed by adults. Infancy and childhood are the periods in life when the self comes closest to enjoying full latitude in satisfying its impulses; from the perspective of adulthood, then, the initial stages of life constitute the Golden Age or, in Biblical terms, the Garden of Eden preceding the time of toil and tribulation. Freud insists that everyone secretly longs for a return to the paradise of infancy; hence the id's quest for perfect pleasure appears in his genetic explanation as the self's inclination to regress toward infancy.

The notion of regression has important implications in psychoanalytic therapy. For instance, an earlier discussion noted that a patient resists restoration of a traumatic event to his conscious-ness thereby indicating that he has repressed, and not just forgotten, the event. Freud holds that the unconsciousness preserves not only the infantile ambition for total happiness but also specific attempts to fulfill this ambition. An example may prove helpful. A nursing infant instinctively tries to establish an indestructible union with the mother's breast because the breast gratifies its immediate need for food. But when the infant finally passes the nursing stage its attraction to mother's breast may not diminish. In more technical terms, the infant may develop a merely psychological *fixation* with the breast once the biologically inspired and justified attraction has subsided. In trying to break the fixation the mother may resort to punishment, which may precipitate a trauma that will haunt the child during its later life.

The therapeutic significance of fixation concerns its role as an indicator that an individual cannot accept the loss of earlier and therefore more infantile or id-oriented types of pleasure. Fixation represents an inordinately strong resistance against the ineluctable process of growing up and accepting the rigors of adult life. Thus a particular fixation shows the specific way an individual gives in to his regressive tendencies. The literature of popular psychoanalysis abounds with examples. For instance, smokers supposedly suffer from an oral fixation; their regressive search for pleasure involves a return to the oral stage of instinctual gratification. In any case fixations offer the psychoanalyst clues from which he tries to decipher the exact manner in which his patient unconsciously pursues unconditional happiness. The patient's fixations also may lead to the disclosure of those traumas that the patient so effectively represses, for traumas often result from the attempts of parents and others to break early fixations.

Another key notion in the genetic model is the previously mentioned biogenetic law, whose simplest formulation is: ontogenesis (or the maturation of the individual) repeats phylogenesis (or the evolution of the species). Since this law inspires many of Freud's fanciful and even bizarre speculations in anthropology, further discussion of it will occur in the fifth section, "The Oedipal Project, Sublimation, and Civilization." There the Oedipal project will be examined with the aid of all Freud's genetic categories.

One explanatory model remains to be considered. It is called the *organic* model because it is concerned with the advanced capacity for self-regulated growth that sets organisms apart from the rest of nature.[8] This model rewards Freud's search for replacements for some deficient conceptions in his mechanistic analysis of the self. The difference between the two models can be shown with reference to formation of the superego.

Freud's mechanistic account of the superego lends itself to a stimulus-response interpretation. This account emphasizes that the superego originates through the process of introjecting external (usually parental) authority; hence formation of the superego signals a transfer of obligations from external figures of authority to the self. That genesis of the superego coincides with the internalization of parental and other rules invites comparison between man and machine; specifically, the self into which various authorities insert instructions seems comparable to a computer into which technicians put a program. But if so strong an analogical relationship holds between man and machine, Freud's explanation of behavior should translate freely into the jargon of stimulus-response. For example, Freud credits to a well-developed superego the normal adult's restraint in satisfying his urges. An apparently equivalent stimulus-response explanation would attribute the same behavior to conditioning that trains the individual to respond in a particular manner under the influence of specific stimuli; hence the adult usually shows self-control because he has been conditioned to do so.

Freud's mechanistic explanation of the self thus leaves the following impressions. Parents and other authorities manufacture a topographical device, the superego, by inserting instructions into the self. The apparatus takes over from its producers the job of controlling behavior, and, of course, the superego can be improved and strengthened periodically so that its guidance becomes more efficient and inclusive. Significantly, however, construction of the superego brings about no essential change in control of behavior; its completion merely alters the controller's spatial location. Before creation of the superego, controlled behavior constitutes a response (effect) to external stimulation (cause); with its appearance in the self, the source of the controlling stimulation becomes internal. In both cases, though, controlled behavior represents a programmed or conditioned response to specific stimuli.

Freud's organic model of the self centers on the resemblance and continuity between man and other forms of life rather than on the relationship between man and his inorganic creations, such as machines. The organic explanations give emphasis to man's capacity for kinds of self-regulated activity that apparently could not be duplicated with even the most elaborate external conditioning. With respect to formation of the superego, however, the organic account does not contradict its mechanistic counterpart at every turn; for instance, both trace the superego's origin to the introjection of (external) authority. But the organic explanation denies that the superego can be understood merely in terms of stimulus-response conditioning.

A previous discussion mentioned that Freud eventually divides the instincts into two fundamental groups, the Life, or erotic, drives and the Death, or destructive, drives. The discussion also noted that the Death instincts contribute to the preservation of both individual and communal life. For instance, the energy that must be spent in taming the environment for, say, farming comes from the Death instincts. These instincts, however, can serve the interests of survival only if they function under strict supervision; unregulated drives lead only to death. Thus operation of the Death instincts falls under the psychoanalytic maxim that only constrained, controlled, or sublimated instinctual energy works for rather than against life.

If the disciplined Death instincts are given an outward direction (for instance, toward the conquest of nature), then they may promote life. The qualifying verb *may* is not unreasoned. Aiming the energy of the Death instincts away from the self toward the environment provides no guarantee that the effects of this energy will be beneficent. Freud remarks in several places that mankind soon may destroy itself through technological warfare, and war constitutes an obvious case in which energy from the destructive instincts flows outward. Turning the full thurst of the Death instincts away from the self does not represent even the most effective means of harnassing them in the service of life. If some energy from these instincts is turned toward the self, then it can be transformed so that it reduces the very threat to survival that the Death instincts pose. This peculiarity arises because the inwardly directed Death instincts furnish energy for strengthening the superego, which then becomes more active in constraining the self-destructive bent of those instincts. The matter can be clarified further by reviewing the relationship between the id and the superego.

In adult life the main responsibility for controlling the id falls on the superego. According to the organic explanation of the self, however, reciprocity as well as conflict marks the relation between these agencies. Once the superego has been formed through the introjection of (external) authority, its further development does not depend exclusively on reinforcement from the outside; the superego then can influence its own growth by interacting with the id.

The dynamics of the superego's self-regulation can be analyzed in this way. Immediately after its genesis the superego's primary task involves quelling any self-destructive impulse from the id. With regard to the Death instincts, the superego's disciplinary actions fall into two groups. First, the superego allocates some energy from these instincts for useful aggression against the environment, which might involve anything from plowing fields to making war. Second, the superego appropriates some energy from the Death instincts for its own projects; namely, the superego uses energy that it takes from the id in order to extend its dominion over the id. The second type of disciplinary action against the id has well-known effects. Some people, for instance, suffer from an overly scrupulous conscience; they may reproach themselves for harboring desires that others write off as unavoidable. In technical language, such people have a superego that directs against the id too much energy from the Death instincts. Thus the superego becomes too aggressive toward the id by giving excessive amounts of instinctual energy an inward direction. That the superego can make itself a harsh dictator through its appropriation of energy from the id implies that the self has the ability to regulate its own development, which occurs through interaction of the self's own topographical agencies without direct intervention from external sources. In summary, the self exemplifies the quality of self-regulation that all forms of organic existence share.

Freud's organic model also has important political and social implications, which will be discussed soon. First, however, a developmental sketch of his theory about the instincts may provide the best summary of the four models through which he presents the theory.

A Developmental Sketch of the Theory of Instincts

Both the initial and the final categories in Freud's theory of instincts come from literature rather than from natural science. The theory begins with a dualism of Hunger and Love, and it ends with an opposition between Life (Eros) and Death (Thanatos). The choice of terms indicates that the theory derives its inspiration as much from the speculations of poets and philosophers as from the research of scientists and psychotherapists. But the theory's language can be misleading in at least one sense. Psychotherapeutic practice serves as one impetus for the refinement and expansion of the theory; hence Freud never divorces his theory about the instincts from psychoanalytic work with them. Let us trace the movement of his theory from the Love-Hunger rivalry to the Life-Death dualism.

The struggle between Hunger and Love symbolizes the conflict between ego (self-preservation) and sexual (group preservation) drives. This opposition of primary instincts corresponds nicely with the distinction between the reality and pleasure principles. The first antagonist, Hunger, represents the self in efforts to preserve its existence by respecting the dictates of the reality principle; namely, the self modifies its pursuit of pleasure according to the requirements of survival. Hunger promotes food over sex, but the drive may lead the self to ignore the needs of the species. Specifically, the self may become so preoccupied with its own preservation that it abstains from procreating and raising offspring. Thus the second belligerent, Love, promotes the pleasure of sexual intercourse over the difficulties and dangers of having progeny. In this way Love ensures that winning the battle for self-survival will not entail losing the war for survival of the species.

In Freud's initial classification goal or orientation is the criterion for sorting the primary instincts into either ego or sexual uses. Instincts that have the self as their object fall into the ego category; those that have the other (that is, either a specific sexual partner or society at large) as their goal belong in the sexual category. The ego-sexual division therefore rests on the distinction between self-directed and other-directed drives—a point that has an important consequence. The division between ego and sexual instincts cannot be basic unless the distinction between the self and the other also is fundamental, for, again, the ego-sexual dichotomy comes directly from the self-other dualism. Freud's study of infants convinced him that the self-other opposition was not primordial; early infants supposedly draw no distinction between themselves and the objects, including persons, that comprise their environment. Consequently, he concluded that the ego-sexual division of the instincts could not be basic. Some details of his study should be considered.

Perhaps the most striking aspect of any Freudian study is the assumption that sex has a pervasive effect on behavior, and Freud's analysis of infants proves no exception. His investigations of infant sexuality center on the stages through which the newly born allegedly progress. Probably the most familiar stages are the oral, anal, and genital (phallic), so named because of the part of the anatomy that most attracts an infant during different periods of its development. In the oral stage, for instance, the infant's own mouth becomes the main object of its attention. Each stage occurs within the period of autoeroticism that precedes heteroeroticism. The autoerotic self derives (sexual) satisfaction principally from manipulating the oral, anal, or the genital areas of its own body. The heteroerotic self, conversely, has matured to the degree that it seeks (sexual) enjoyment primarily from its interaction with others in either bisexual intercourse or homosexual activity. Freud maintains, however, that a period of primary narcissism antedates even autoeroticism, and to distinguish the two periods he appeals to putative facts about psychological development. For the sake of clarification it is assumed that Freud is right about these facts so that their relevance to the ego-sexual division may be discussed.

During each autoerotic stage the self can make relatively advanced discriminations among the objects that fall within its sensory field; otherwise it could not show preference for a particular organ such as its mouth. The autoerotic self also draws the more general distinction between itself and its environment, including other selves. At least in principle, then, the ego-sexual division of instincts may apply in the autoerotic self, for such division presupposes only the distinction between the self and the other. Prior to autoeroticism the self's drives cannot be so classified because the self has not yet set up the boundaries that separate self from other. Thus the period of primary narcissism extends from birth to the infant's recognition of itself as a distinct entity—exactly the period of time in which the self has not yet distinguished itself from the other. Since the division between ego (self-directed) and sexual (other-directed) instincts collapses apart from the self-other distinction, the division cannot be original or primary.

The phenomenon of primary narcissism implies the unoriginality of the ego-sexual division of instincts in that it indicates the absence of separate ego instincts during earliest infancy. But the study of primary narcissism confirms Freud's thesis that every drive has a sexual quality; hence the phenomenon undermines the primacy of the ego instincts but not of the sexual instincts. Two considerations should help to clarify the point. First, the theory of instincts often equates instinctual drives with sexual drives. In the equation, however, sexuality must be interpreted broadly so that it covers everything from infantile narcissism to ordinary copulation. Second, the instincts encounter least resistance during the earlier stages of life; hence strong domination by instinctual or sexual (in the broad sense) drives characterizes the period of primary narcissism. Freud's analysis of the phenomenon therefore leads him to defend the originality or primacy of the sexual instincts and to concede the derivative nature of the ego instincts.

The first major revision in the theory of instincts now can be summarized. The earliest stages of infancy form the period of primary narcissim in which the self behaves as a sexual solipsist; during that period it remains oblivious to the difference between itself and the other. If the self-other distinction is unoriginal, however, so is the division of instincts into ego or self-directed and sexual or other-directed categories. Thus the reputed fact of primary narcissism implies that an undifferentiated libido (sexual, instinctual drive) predates separate ego and sexual instincts.

An impressive continuity marks the transition from the initial opposition between Hunger and Love to the final struggle between Death and Life. All of the intermediate states in Freud's theory need not be delineated here; rather, discussion concentrates on his reasons for capping the theory with the struggle between Life and Death. First, however, consideration should be given to his view that two primary instincts must exist.

Freud calls his own theory of instincts a dualism in distinguishing it from such alternative doctrines as Jung's monism. His dualism has three major tenets. First, the self contains two coeval primary instincts; its reservoir of energy therefore must be divided between two sets of drives. Second, the primary instincts stand in ultimate opposition to each other; hence they cause disharmony in the self. Third, the struggle between the primary instincts ends only with death, although death does not necessarily signal the victory of one (Death) over the other (Life). Freud rarely presents a formal defense of the thesis that the primary instincts number two instead of one because it strikes him as self-evidently true. Data from psychotherapy, history, and common sense support the conclusion that human life involves a predominance of pain over pleasure, frustration over satisfaction, conflict over reconciliation—unhappy conditions that apparently do not confine themselves to particular regions, cultures, or epochs but seem to be the universal fate of man. Freud's dualism represents the foundation of his theory about these ordinary and depressing facts. Since the conflict between the primary instincts belongs to the very structure of the id, and since the id never varies in essence, the self exists in a state of permanent instinctual disharmony. Thus the dualism of the instincts reflects Freud's pessimism about man's condition.

As the theory of instincts approaches a final version, the dualism becomes more pronounced until it culminates in the opposition between Life and Death. This trend in the theory mirrors Freud's search for an alternative to the ego or self-preservation instinct. As noted earlier, the phenomenon of primary narcissism breaks the ego-sexual dualism because it shows that an undifferentiated sexual drive (libido) antedates a separate ego instinct; consequently it reduces the initial dualism to a monism of the sexual instinct. After his studies on primary narcissism Freud, the inveterate dualist, had to find a replacement for the ego instinct, and he eventually settled on Thanatos or the Death instinct. A review of psychotherapeutic evidence that aided him in the selection is in order.

Previous allusions to the Death instinct have noted only two of its functions. First, the outwardly directed Death instinct supplies energy for activities ranging from agriculture to war. The Death instinct's role in all of these activities is labeled simply its *outward aggression*. Second, the inwardly directed Death instinct contributes energy to the superego's battle against the id's pursuit of absolute pleasure; if the superego wins too decisively it may become an overly scrupulous conscience. The Death instinct's function in this regard is called its *inward aggression*. Originally Freud did not posit the existence of a Death instinct in order to explain either outward or inward aggression; instead, he was led to assume the presence of Thanatos on the basis of a strategy that patients often adopt in trying to stop an analyst's probings. This defense mechanism reveals a compulsion to repeat; and compulsive repetition betrays the operation of a primordial Death instinct. Perhaps an example will provide the best clarification of Freud's thinking on the matter.

Assume that a patient, X, developed a fixation for his mother's breast during childhood; namely, the duration or intensity of his psychological attachment to the breast exceeded the normal biological attraction that aids the nursing infant. This fixation represents the id's delaying action against the process of growing up. The id takes such action because its domination of the self declines as the self matures, for as the self grows older it discards the pure pleasure principle that governs the id in favor of the reality principle. X's fixation therefore constitutes an infantile, unrealistic attempt to halt his inevitable march toward adulthood and is, as well, a specific example of the regressive behavior through which the self tries to restore an earlier and therefore more id-oriented and pleasurable period of life. Hence the fixation illustrates the self's resistance to outgrowing an original source of pleasure.

The example requires an additional assumption in order to exhibit the notion of compulsive repetition. Accordingly, assume also that in trying to break his son's fixation X's father resorted to punishment which, in turn, lead to X's longstanding feeling of resentment toward his father. Finally, X represses all of these events in the deepest recesses of his unconsciousness. His psychoanalyst's first task involves making X aware of the trauma he is suppressing. But X resists therapy with the strategy of transference. Instead of simply recalling the unhappy episodes of his childhood, X attempts in effect to relive them; namely, he confronts the psychotherapist with the same hateful attitude he originally developed against his father. In short, X acts as if the analyst were his father. By this transference of feeling X transforms a past trauma into a present event; he substitutes the *repetition* of his childhood for its simple *recall*. If X were merely to remember the trauma and the pleasurable periods of life that preceded it, then he would have to recognize the unrepeatable character of his past. Through the stratagem of transference he can act as if the past were not gone forever but, rather, repeatable indefinitely. For Freud, then, the phenomenon of transference indicates the self's refusal to completely abandon the pleasures and even the traumas of its strongly id-oriented past. The act of transference shows that the self suffers from a compulsion to repeat (relive) its own past.

Freud adduces evidence for compulsive repetition from ordinary as well as pathological examples; for instance, people who persistently call misfortune on themselves, who seem to be born losers, supposedly exemplify the same symptoms as those of the transferring patient. The most interesting point at present, though, concerns Freud's attempt to deduce the existence of the Death instinct from the phenomenon of compulsive repetition. His argument is this. Compulsive repetition constitutes the self's effort to conserve its own past with more than memory; that is, past events are reconstructed and relived (as against just remembered). But the self's attempt to repeat its own past does not take place at a rational level; indeed, to call the repetition compulsive is to suggest that it must originate in the instincts rather than in reason.

Once the instinctual foundation for compulsive repetition has been secured, Freud's argument needs only one more premise in order to demonstrate that the Death instinct supplies that foundation. The premise seems incontrovertible; it states simply that the inorganic is the prior state of the organic. The self clearly qualifies as an organic being, and it possesses a drive to restore earlier stages of its development through more than memory; so the ultimate goal must be the self's own death, for only through death can the self return to its original, inanimate existence. Freud expresses this conclusion with the slogan, "The aim of all life is death," and he offers the following summation of his argument.

> But how is the predicate of being "instinctual" related to the compulsion to repeat? At this point we cannot escape a suspicion that we may have come upon the track of a universal attribute of instincts and perhaps of organic life in general which has not been recognized clearly or at least not stressed explicitly to this point. *It seems, then, that an instinct is an urge inherent in organic life to restore an earlier state of things* which the living entity has been obliged to abandon under the pressure of external distrubing forces; that is, it is a kind of organic elasticity or, to put it another way, the expression of the inertia inherent in organic life.[10]

After arguing that the phenomenon of compulsive repetition implies the presence of a Death instinct in the self, Freud offers an even more startling thesis. He says that Thanatos replaces the ego or self-preservation instinct in the original ego-sexual dualism. The new dualism pits Death against Eros, which now takes the place of the sexual or group-preservation instinct. The thesis becomes less paradoxical on inspection. Under the direction of Thanatos the self seeks only a "natural" death; it resists every *external* threat against its existence. One example from medicine and another from common sense illustrate the point. That the body generates a physiological resistance against such germs as the diphtheria bacillus, a death-dealing bacterium, seems to offer evidence against operation of a Death instinct in the self, but the body mounts such a defense precisely because the germ represents an external threat to its survival. Hence the self tries to counteract the bacterium so that it can return to a "natural" course of dying. Similarly, that human beings normally resist assault does not belie the existence of a Death instinct; instead it indicates that death from external violence does not count as a "natural" form of dying.

The thesis that the Death instinct functions as a self-preservation drive remains implausible until the key notion of a "natural" death has been satisfactorily explained. In providing the required clarification Freud calls on two notions from the earlier theory of instincts: the pleasure principle and the mechanistic equation of pleasure with reduced tension. The unharnessed id operates under the (pure) pleasure principle because it strives after the immediate and complete gratification of its impulses. Such gratification would bring perfect pleasure, but the tenets of Freud's mechanistic model imply that the living self never can experience absolute pleasure. This conclusion follows from two principles. First, tension (disequilibrium) as such detracts from pleasure; hence perfect pleasure equals the total reduction of tension. Second, life alternates continuously between states of produced and reduced tension; consequently life without disequilibrium is impossible. The principles jointly entail that life itself brings insurmountable pain (absence of pleasure), and death alone can ensure unconditional pleasure through the full and everlasting elimination of tension.

The equation of life with unending pain provides the background for Freud's ingenious answer to the question of what counts as a "natural" death. Thanatos seeks a "natural" death for the self precisely in that it strives after the absolute pleasure that only the quietude of the grave can provide. Since the very nature of an instinct impels its pursuit after absolute pleasure, and since such pleasure comes solely with death, it seems quite appropriate for Freud to posit the existence of a Death instinct. Finally, to claim that the Death instinct functions in effect as a self-preservation drive is merely to say that it resists noninstinctual (external, unnatural) causes of death. Thanatos protects the self from outside threats to life so that the self may die under the guidance of Thanatos itself.

The notion of a primary Death drive has repercussions throughout the theory of instincts, especially with respect to the distinction between the pleasure and reality principles. If the (pure) pleasure principle governs the id, and if the id contains a primary instinct that pursues a natural death for the self, then the pleasure principle can be called the Nirvana principle, a name that emphasizes the mechanistic equation of unconditional pleasure with the tranquility of death.[11] Yet the identification of pleasure with Nirvana apparently undermines the dualism of the instincts. The later theory of instincts replaces the ego-sexual dichotomy with the Life-Death division. If the Nirvana principle reigns in the id, though, then presumably all of its drives must be directed toward the final elimination of tension, or death. Thus the identification in question seems to leave Freud with a monism of the Death instinct. Further, the claim that Nirvana represents perfect pleasure breaks the continuity between the (pure) pleasure principle and the reality principle. The last point requires clarification.

The early theory of instincts states the relationship that holds between the pleasure and reality principles. The unsupervised id operates according to the (pure) pleasure principle because it seeks instantaneous and full satisfaction of its urges. This course of action can lead to death alone because absolute pleasure remains incompatible with life. Thus the ego, in an alliance with the superego, brings the id's drives under the regulation of the reality principle, which allows only their partial and delayed gratification. By attempting to harness the id with rational control, the ego offers a compromise between pleasure and life; namely, life under the reality principle requires only the disciplined pursuit rather than the total rejection of pleasure. In this light the reality principle appears as the rationally or realistically amended version of the pleasure principle; hence the reality principle could be called the *restrained* as against the *pure* pleasure principle.

Freud's equation of pleasure with Nirvana (death) destroys the relationship of compatibility between pleasure and reality (life). If pleasure ultimately coincides with death, then life must be intrinsically painful. Stated somewhat differently, the equation of pleasure with Nirvana implies that a fundamental antagonism rather than a difference in emphasis separates the pleasure and reality principles. The later theory of instincts affirms this antagonism by elevating the reality principle to a special status. After the appearance of the Death instinct and the transformation of pleasure into Nirvana, reality ceases to be just another principle. Together with the two basic instincts, it receives a special title, *Ananke*, which can be translated ''Reality'' but also connotes ''scarcity,'' ''destiny,'' and even ''nature.''

Freud's introduction of the Greek name signals an important shift in the theory of instincts. Specifically, his use of the term has two major implications. First, Reality now belongs to the triumvirate that rules the self; the other two members are the primary instincts, Eros and Thanatos. Second, Reality stands in direct opposition to its fellow triumvirs; they govern from within the self while Ananke represents foreign domination. As Ananke, then, Reality does not constitute one of the two principles the id may follow in its pursuit of pleasure; Reality becomes an external force that impedes and frustrates the id's effort to satisfy its urges. Reality in the role of Ananke opposes rather than simply regulates the id.

An ironical twist occurs during the development of Freud's

theory about the instincts. His studies on primary narcissism leave open one slot in the original ego-sexual division of primary instincts, because these studies allegedly show that an undifferentiated libido (sexual drive) antedates separate ego and sexual instincts. This change in the theory of instincts can be summarized: a monism of the sexual instinct replaces an ego-sexual dualism. Freud then suggests that Thanatos can fill the vacancy in the initial dualism. He justifies the nomination on the grounds that both the Death and the ego instincts function as self-preservation drives. Since Thanatos seeks only a natural death for the self, it protects the self from external (noninstinctual) threats against life and thus promotes survival. This stage in the theory of instincts can be characterized: Death-sexual dualism replaces the monism of the sexual instinct.

The very evidence that supports the presence of a Death instinct, though, also undermines the new dualism. The existence of a Death drive follows from the self's impulse to relive earlier periods of its existence. Since the self as an organism comes ultimately from inorganic matter, its compulsion to retreat toward the past constitutes a drive to die. The point can be expressed in different terms. The Death instinct obeys the psychoanalytic law that all drives have pleasure as their goal. According to the mechanistic account of the self, pleasure results directly and exclusively from a reduction of tension; so the quest for pleasure coincides with the drive for a natural death, because death alone completely eliminates tension. Thus the pleasure principle, under which the entire id operates, equals the Nirvana principle; that is, *all* instincts seek death precisely because they all pursue absolute pleasure. The corresponding shift in the theory of instincts is: a monism of the Death instinct replaces the Death-sexual dualism. Ironically, then, discovery of the Death instinct does not transform the monism of the sexual instinct into a viable dualism but, instead, generates a new monism of Thanatos.

The purpose of this condensed review has been to underscore

Freud's difficulty in anchoring the final theory of instincts in a secure dualism. In his attempt to avoid the new monism of Thanatos he substitutes for the sexual instinct Eros, whose problematical nature is considered in the remainder of this section.

Of the many possible translations of the term *Eros*, the most common probably are "desire" and "love," with strong accent on the sexual connotations of these words. Freud's use of the term draws on its rich associations with Greek mythology. In the Orphic tales about the origin of the cosmos, for example, Eros acts as a force behind the sexual relations that produce the immortal gods. Within the theory of instincts Eros retains the function of a unifying force. It has the same job as the earlier sexual instincts; namely, it serves as a group-preservation instinct by establishing durable and expanding social relationships. Under the guise of sexual passion, for instance, Eros leads to procreation; then it binds members of the family together with mutual affection so that the offspring will enjoy the security necessary for survival. In a similar way Eros promotes the formation of larger social units such as the community and even the nation. But in order to justify his claim that Eros qualifies as a primary instinct, Freud must solve two problems.

After arguing for the existence of Thanatos, Freud offers this definition of an instinct: "An instinct is an urge inherent in organic life to restore an earlier state of things." The definition fits the Death instinct quite nicely, since Thanatos strives to restore the inorganic state from which the self originally came; but only a strained version of the definition applies to Eros, and Freud himself concedes the criticism. He claims that bisexual intercourse may be the most obvious manifestation of Eros, and he appeals to Plato's *Symposium* to indicate it can be construed as an urge "to restore an earlier state of things." In this dialog Aristophanes proposes the fanciful thesis that Zeus made the male and female sexes by splitting apart a third, androgynous sex. Bisexual intercourse represents an effort to restore the third sex and, therefore, "an earlier state of things." Freud grants that this story lends little support to the claim that

Eros fits his new definition of an instinct; indeed, he almost apologizes for relating the tale.[12]

Another equally serious objection can be brought against the claim that Eros qualifies as a primary instinct. As an instinct Eros must operate according to the pleasure principle. The equation of pleasure with Nirvana, however, implies that the entire id (namely, every instinct) strives after the tranquility of death (that is, perfect pleasure). If Eros seeks death, then it becomes virtually indistinguishable from Thanatos. If Eros does not seek death, then it apparently does not qualify as an instinct, because all instincts pursue pleasure (death).

This dilemma can be expressed in slightly different language. The final theory of instincts introduces a rigid either-or relationship between pleasure and life by turning the reality principle into Ananke. In the earlier theory the self could have both pleasure and life by governing the id with the reality, or restrained pleasure, principle. In the later theory, however, Reality stands in irreconcilable conflict with the instincts, thereby forfeiting its role as one of the principles that can regulate them. If Reality directly opposes the instincts in their search for pleasure, men evidently the self must choose between pleasure and survival. Thus the final theory of instincts seems to offer strict equations between (a) pleasure and death and (b) pain and life. Eros defies both equations. If it qualifies as an instinct, then Eros, too, must seek pleasure (death). But in order to remain distinct from the Death drive Eros must pursue life (pain); yet if it seeks pain, then presumably Eros cannot be an instinct.

Freud tries to circumvent this difficulty by broadening the mechanistic conception of pleasure. He suggests that some kinds of pleasure do not involve a simple reduction of tension; hence the pursuit of pleasure cannot be equated with the quest for Nirvana. If at least two types of pleasure exist, both Eros and Thanatos can meet the minimal definition of an instinct (namely, an automatic and a nonrational drive for pleasure) without losing their respective identities. Clearly, however, this resolution of the problem demands a convincing clarification of the new, nonmechanistic kind of pleasure; Freud must explain in detail how Eros can pursue pleasure without pursuing death (Nirvana). In Chapter 7 it is argued that he makes no satisfactory distinction between pleasure and Nirvana; further, such a distinction would undercut one of his best insights into civilization. At present it suffices to note that Freud has difficulty in defending Eros as a primary instinct.[13]

The evolution of Freud's theory about the instincts from the ego-sexual dualism to the opposition between Thanatos and Eros has been traced; the way data from practical psychoanalysis influenced the theory's development has been noted; and problems with its final formulation have been considered. The time has come to indicate how the theory of instincts doubles as a theory of civilization.

The Oedipal Project, Sublimation, and Civilization

No aspect of psychoanalysis invites more controversy than the Oedipal complex. The notion deserves the attention and even much of the ridicule it receives; its importance in psychoanalysis can hardly be exaggerated. The most telling criticisms concern Freud's thesis that the complex explains the literal origin of civilization as well as the fate of each human being. Freud believes that the Oedipal struggle falls under the biogenetic law; hence the struggle reportedly plays a role in the development of both society and its members. Freud makes the story of Oedipus (Electra) into an account of civilization by constructing a myth about the primal horde, which will be considered shortly.[14] A matter of interpretation, though, should be settled at the outset.

No defense will be offered for two of the three major functions the Oedipal complex performs in Freudian theory. The first concerns its status as a (putative) law of developmental psychology; namely, each person supposedly acquires the complex during childhood.

The second involves its significance as a hypothesis of empirical anthropology: the complex allegedly accounts for the transition from patriarchal despotism to primitive democracy. Finally, the story of Oedipus symbolizes the conflict between happiness and civilization. Freud's critics usually consider the first two functions of the complex at the expense of the third, because many psychologists and anthropologists dispute the accuracy of the Oedipal theory with respect to their own fields. This discussion, however, concerns the relation between psychoanalysis and unhappiness; hence only the last role of the Oedipal story will be considered here. For the sake of both brevity and prudence, the other aspects of the story will be thrown for evaluation to Freud's critics.

The details in Freud's Oedipal theory can be outlined as follows. The complex, the toughest obstacle along the path from infancy to adulthood, arises when the male (female) child develops a strong sexual attraction for its mother (father). The incestuous wish accords with the child's primary drives; that is, sexual intercourse with its mother would gratify the child's erotic urges. Such an act also would satisfy the Death instinct's search for absolute pleasure (Nirvana) in the final release of tension. The child's wish to copulate with mother indicates its regression toward the security of the womb and, ultimately, the tranquility of its original inorganic existence. In more prosaic language, the child's desire to sleep with its mother represents an infantile and unrealistic demand for perfect contentment, and only its death could provide such contentment. Consequently, the child's incestuous impulse must be stifled in the interest of its survival. Freud says that the father normally undertakes the task of protecting the (male) child from its own self-destructive urges; that is, the father usually plays the unpopular but necessary role of disciplinarian.

Since the father frustrates his child's Oedipal urge, antagonism and resentment begin to mar interaction between the two. From the child's viewpoint the father appears as a barrier to pleasure (namely, sexual involvement with mother), but the father sees his child's incestuous drive as a threat not only to his exclusive sexual right as a husband but also to the child's own maturation. Yet the relationship between the father and his child does not deteriorate entirely. As the child grows older its attitude toward the father becomes increasingly ambivalent; it continues to resent the father's discipline and punishment but also starts to respect the father's power and to appreciate his protection. This ambivalence signals formation of the child's superego, with which the child can impose control over its own urges. In more precise terms, the child's introjection of parental authority forms the superego, which then constrains the id and serves as the ego's ideal or model. The Oedipal conflict enters a new stage when the child pays its father the ultimate compliment of imitation by disciplining its own infantile desires.

Freud uses the Oedipus story both ingeniously and outrageously in his anthropological speculations, which culminate in the myth of the primal horde. Primitive peoples supposedly lived in small groups dominated by a despotic male. The tyrant drove away his sons so that he could keep all of the tribe's women for himself. The exiled brothers retaliated by slaying the hated father and, as a gesture of their newly acquired and shared authority, consuming the father in a cannibalistic orgy. Almost immediately after, however, the brothers became remorseful as the old hatred for their father gave way to mixed feelings; so they introduced rites and rules in order to expiate their crime and alleviate their guilt. With regard to marital relationships, for instance, the brothers set up rigid exogamic codes. By forcing themselves to marry outside the horde they remained obedient to their father, who had forbidden them to have sexual intercourse with the tribe's own women. Thus the brothers betrayed their bloody revolution in two ways. First, they introjected their slain father's commands, thereby forming (strengthening)[15] their consciences, which then rebuked them for liberating themselves through patricide. Second, the brothers elevated these harsh commands to the status of official and permanent laws, thereby replacing a despot with a system of social tyranny.

Details in the myth of the primal horde correspond roughly with the phases in the child's Oedipal struggle. Both the myth and the struggle illustrate the Freudian doctrine that civilization rests on a foundation of denied pleasure. In the individual Oedipal struggle, for instance, the father frustrates his child's incestuous impulse, thereby preventing the child from pursuing the self-destructive search for absolute pleasure or Nirvana. The father also promotes formation of the superego, which represents the child's membership card in society. The superego serves as a socializing force because it brings the child's own control of its behavior into harmony with the demands and expectations of society. Thus the child's admission into society coincides with its self-propelled flight from absolute pleasure. The primal horde story expresses the same point in a more obvious fashion.

The expelled sons must kill their father in order to gain the pleasure (namely, the tribal women) he denies them. Even after his death, however, the tyrant ironically continues his domination as, acting from feelings of guilt and respect, his sons institute regulations that forbid them to marry within the tribe. But in an obvious way the brothers' self-denial differs from their father's control over them. The father's refusal to share the tribal women is blatantly selfish and arbitrary; he tries to monopolize pleasure through the exercise of raw power. His sons, however, transform this tyranny into law by formulating an exogamic code, which they scrupulously obey. According to Freud, the inauguration of such regulatory devices as law and code marks the transition from primitivism to civilization. Thus the brothers create civilization with their *law* against pleasure in the form of intercourse with the tribal women.

The thesis that civilization presupposes a loss of happiness can be stated in a less symbolic fashion by using the notion of sublimation. Freud defines sublimation as the "diversion of sexual instinctual forces from sexual aims and their direction to new ones."[16] Examples of sublimation range from walking the dog to writing a symphony; the process underlies almost every kind of behavior. Freud's definition touches two important points in the theory of instincts: first, it notes the close connection between the sexual and the instinctual; second, it stresses that instinctual energy can be deflected from its original goal toward another goal. These points will be considered in order.

As noted earlier, Freud uses the adjective *sexual* as a near-synonym for the term *instinctual*. The close connection between the words throws light on the meaning of each. The phrase *sexual pleasure* describes a feeling that results from the momentarily complete satisfaction of an intense urge, and Freud chooses sexual pleasure as his paradigm precisely because the instincts pursue absolute pleasure—the full and immediate gratification of a drive. To characterize sexual pleasure as paradigmatic is to suggest that the instincts cannot be fully satisfied once they aim at other than sexual goals.

An example may be helpful. Those who admire great art sometimes talk about the "higher" or "more refined" enjoyment that comes from the creation or contemplation of a masterpiece. Freud does not quarrel with the suggestion that pleasure has many gradations, and he concedes the legitimacy of the higher-lower distinction for classifying pleasures; but he denies that "higher" means "better." Since an activity produces pleasure in direct proportion with its gratification of a drive, the "lower" (namely, the more instinctual or sexual) kinds of pleasure are "better," for they provide relatively full satisfaction of instinctual needs. Sublimation therefore entails a diminution in pleasure because it diverts instinctual energy away from sexual (lower) toward other (higher) goals. The point can be summarized by saying that sublimation diminishes pleasure through its deflection of the instincts.

The relation between sublimation and civilization now can be explained with reference to two familiar facts. First, building and maintaining civilization requires unpleasant work, or toil, which implies that man must pay for civilization with some unhappiness. Technically, civilization's requirements oppose the inclination of the instincts; the necessity of toil runs counter to the drive for pleasure. The conflict between civilization and happiness becomes more evident in light of the second fact; namely, man has only a limited amount of (instinctual) energy, which implies that the self cannot reach a *mutually satisfactory* compromise between pleasure and toil. Since the instincts continuously strive after absolute pleasure in the form of Nirvana (death), their complete gratification would consume all of the self's energy; hence energy can be appropriated for toil only by deflecting the instincts from their natural goal of perfect pleasure. The point can be summarized by saying that civilization requires sublimation. It now follows that civilization diminishes pleasure in that it presupposes the sublimation or deflection of the instincts. Freud states the conclusion this way.

> We believe that civilization has been created under the pressure of the exigencies of life at the cost of satisfaction of the instincts; and we believe that civilization is to a large extent being constantly created anew, since each individual who makes a fresh entry into human society repeats this sacrifice of instinctual satisfaction for the benefit of the whole community.[17]

This analysis of sublimation has been conducted at a general level without mention of specific societies. The omission of examples serves at least one purpose in showing that Freud's account of sublimation supports a theory of civilization that claims universal applicability. The theory's central tenet states that the same process—sublimation—that builds and preserves civilization also detracts from happiness, and it acknowledges no difference between primitive and modern, capitalist and socialist, affluent and impoverished societies. Freud's pessimism covers civilization as such.

The Radicalism and Conservatism of the Instincts

This chapter has tried to locate Freud's pessimistic theory about civilization within his theory of instincts. Perhaps the best way to recapitulate the discussion consists in sketching a topic whose details will be considered in Chapter 7.

Freud describes the instincts as intrinsically conservative, but he cautions that they often appear quite radical. The conservatism stems from a regressive inclination, and Thanatos manifests the most obvious tendency "to restore an earlier state of things" because it pursues Nirvana, or the state of tensionless existence that both precedes and succeeds life itself. In any case the instincts acquire a reputation for radicalism because their quest after absolute pleasure threatens to undermine civilization, which must rest on a foundation of toil and other denied pleasure. Even the most efficient system of suppression cannot eliminate the threat that the instincts pose for civilization because they spring from the timeless, inalterable id. Yet the radicalism of the instincts promotes regress as progress; namely, the instincts seek to improve the future only through permanent restoration of the precivilized, inorganic past. Freud offers this statement of how a real conservatism underlies the apparent radicalism of the instincts.

> Instincts are bound to give a deceptive appearance of being forces tending toward change and progress, while in fact they are merely seeking to reach an ancient goal by paths old and new alike. Moreover, it is possible to specify this final goal of all organic striving. It would be in contradiction to the conservative nature of the instincts if the goal of life were a state of things which had never yet been attained. On the contrary, it must be an *old* state of things, an initial state from which the living entity has at one time or other departed and to which it is striving to return by the circuitous routes along which it develops. . . . These circuitous paths to death, faithfully kept to by the conservative instincts, would thus present us today with the picture of the phenomena of life. If we firmly maintain the exclusively conservative nature of instincts, we cannot arrive at any other notions as to the origin and aim of life.[18]

7
Freud and
the Limited Prospects of
Psychotherapy

Theoretical Pessimism and Practical Optimism

Chapter 6 began with a discussion of the tension between theory and practice (therapy) in psychoanalysis. The theme again has relevance as it bears on the contrast between the ominous conclusions from the theory of instincts and the implicit hope in the practice of psychotherapy. The theory of instincts has highly pessimistic implications because it equates the force behind civilization with the very process that subverts happiness: sublimation of the id's primordial and inalterable drives. The theory implies that instinctual renunciation is a precondition for communal life and therefore survival itself. Although society offers security as a replacement for denied pleasure, the loss in happiness or pleasure that attends even the partial frustration of the instincts cannot be compensated. Freudian theory therefore posits an irreconcilable antagonism between the desire for absolute happiness and the exigencies of civilization survival. Man simply must endure unhappiness as the price of life.

Apparently the pessimism of theoretical psychoanalysis cannot eradicate the tacit optimism in psychoanalytic therapy. Assuming the sincerity of both analyst and patient, even an attempt at psychotherapy implies the belief that man's condition can be improved; otherwise, practical psychoanalysis makes no sense. Since the very effort to alleviate unhappiness indicates hope for the future, psychotherapy retains an optimistic air even without promising a total cure; as long as practical psychoanalysis offers any chance for betterment it evidently stands in opposition to its theoretical counterpart.

The task of the present chapter now can be outlined. Sharp discord seems to exist between the theory of instincts and practical psychoanalysis. The theory states that the instincts remain unregenerate despite every effort at their control, while the need to tame them represents an equally permanent requirement of civilization-survival; hence man's fate consists in an endless clash between his drives and the forces that contain them. But psychoanalytic practice seems to promise an end to the clash, or at least significant movement in that direction; so the question arises whether and how this apparent conflict between the two parts of psychoanalysis can be resolved. This chapter seeks to remove the semblance of conflict by clarifying the sense in which practical psychoanalysis can be called *optimistic*. First, however, the principal features of Freudian therapy should be discussed.

Psychoanalysis as an Exercise in Interpretation

The view that dreams should not be dismissed as nocturnal curiosities did not originate with Freud, but his proposals for decoding them represents the first promising attempt to secure a truly scientific method of interpretation. Freud's interest in dreams stems from the conviction that they contain inscriptions written in the language of desire. In more prosaic terms, dreams reportedly provide access to wishes and frustrations that usually remain repressed during waking life. The initial task of practical psychoanalysis consists in deciphering both the patient's account of his dreams and the dreams themselves; the immediate aim of such analysis is to penetrate the otherwise hidden recesses of the patient's unconsciousness. The final goal of the analysis will be considered shortly; but some difficulties that beset the interpretation of dreams should be mentioned first.[1]

Dreams have two principal strata. One contains the manifest content or literal significance of the dream, and the other comprises its latent content or underlying meaning. An example from Freud's cases may be instructive. A married woman dreams about giving a dinner party, but she has only smoked salmon to serve. She cannot shop because the stores have closed for the day, and she cannot call a caterer because the telephone suddenly has gone out of order. The woman therefore abandons the plan. These details belong to the dream's manifest content, and their interpretation discloses its latent content. Freud attempts to gather additional data for his analysis by questioning the patient, and her responses provide the following information. On the day before the dream the woman visited a thin female friend whom her husband admires; the woman's jealousy, however, is tempered by the knowledge that her spouse likes a buxom figure. During the visit the friend remarked that she wished to put on weight, and she added that another invitation to enjoy the woman's fine cooking therefore would be welcome. Finally, the woman knows that her friend prefers smoked salmon to any other dish. Thus the dream's latent content is a jealous woman's adversion to aiding a rival for her husband's affection; although the manifest content reports her inability to give a dinner party, the dream really indicates her firm opposition to a project that may make her rival even more attractive to her husband.

Freud tries to explain the need for the interpretation of dreams by investigating their origin. He regards the manifest content as the product of various kinds of (unconscious) dream work, which may draw on varied sources, from vivid recent events to purely imaginary objects or occurrences, for its raw materials. (On the day before her dream, for instance, the woman heard a suggestion that she give a dinner party.) The materials in the manifest content, though, differ from ordinary mental images because they have been invested with thoughts and feelings that comprise the latent content. (The woman's futile efforts to arrange a dinner party symbolize her desire not to help a rival.) Perhaps the best clarification for dream work and its products consists in examining two kinds.

The process of condensation compresses thoughts and feelings of the latent content into a smaller number of items in the manifest content. For instance, a single individual in the manifest content may combine characteristics of several people. In a young man's dream a collective person might be the woman who resembles both his mother and his fiancée. As a result of condensation the manifest content becomes overdetermined; that is, each item in it has multiple meanings (interpretations) because it expresses a variety of thoughts and feelings or because it represents several persons or events. A second kind of dreamwork is called *displacement*, a term that refers to the process that detaches an emotion or attitude from its true object as it attaches it to an apparently unrelated object. A simple illustration is a boy who resents his father and dreams about injuring a friend against whom he bears no grudge.

In general, dreamwork constructs (a) the manifest content out of (b) raw materials such as memories and (c) repressed thoughts and feelings that constitute the latent content. More precisely, the manifest content results from injecting (b) with (c). Composition of the manifest content therefore entails the disguising and distortion of the latent content through such devices as condensation and displacement, which implies that discovery of the latent content requires a process that undoes the accomplishments of dreamwork. In short, the interpretation of dreams coincides with their decomposition or analysis. The psychoanalyst's task thus involves the reversal of the dreamwork that transforms (b) and (c) into (a)—reversal that may demand, say, the dissection of a collective person into the constituent individuals.

The main issue here, however, concerns Freud's explanation about why dreams must be decomposed or interpreted at all. The most obvious response is that the analysis or interpretation of dreams must offset their synthesis or composition. But question then arises about the cause behind the work that composes a dream in the first place. Freud's answer to this query calls on a familiar theme in theoretical psychoanalysis; namely, dreamwork represents an (unconscious) effort to repress desires and the problems (traumas) associated with their frustration. In different terms, dreamwork protects the self even in sleep from both the insatiable demands of the instincts and the unhappy experiences that stem from refusal of those demands. Another look at Freud's views on the instincts should clarify the matter.

Since the instincts lie in the extreme depths of the unconsciousness they remain inaccessible to direct inspection. Even during sleep, when the self's repressive apparatus becomes relatively relaxed, its drives can be known only indirectly. Yet in order to gain even this indirect or inferential knowledge, elaborate techniques of interpretation must be applied to whatever clues about the instincts happen to be available. Simply, the instincts can be known only through the interpretation or analysis of their manifestations. Dreams furnish one set of data from which the nature of the instincts, together with the history of their inhibition, can be inferred, but other evidence is available. Freud maintains that both primitive culture and certain familiar aspects of waking life (for instance, the so-called Freudian slip) offer additional information about the instincts.[2]

Because the instincts can be known only inferentially, the *uninterpreted* manifest content of a dream does not disclose their true character. Conversely, that the therapist tries to analyze his patient's dream implies that its manifest content presents only a disguised and distorted picture of the instincts. A good interpretation sufficiently corrects the distortion so that an educated guess can be made about what lies behind the disguise. The analysis of dreams, though, never can yield more than indirect acquaintance with the id; so no interpretation of a dream can be covered with a guarantee of absolute accuracy. The conclusion that a particular manifest content discloses specific information about the instincts and their inhibition always remains hypothetical. The woman's dream about the dinner party may reveal her secret jealousy, but it also may indicate something altogether different.

The study of both dreams and other clues about the instincts merely initiates the Freudian program of psychotherapy. An example may prove helpful in pointing out some ensuing steps of the treatment. Assume that an analyst's interpretation of his patient's dreams leads to a diagnosis of acute masochism. With reference to Freud's organic and topographical models of the self, this condition arises because the patient's superego has given an inward bent to an inordinate amount of energy from the Death instinct so that the self has become overly aggressive and hostile toward its own (instinctual) ambitions for happiness. Metaphorically, the superego has answered the id's incessant demands for pleasure with a dictatorial refusal and severe disciplinary action. Early in the attempted cure the patient himself receives an explanation of the illness aimed at encouraging him to readjust, through his ego, the unhealthy relation between his id and his superego. Specifically, the patient's ego must be persuaded to undercut the superego's tyranny so that the energy the superego takes from the Death instinct does not continue to threaten the welfare of the entire self; the ego must restrain the superego from channeling so much (instinctual) energy in an inward direction.

This discussion can be translated into less technical language. Improvement of the masochistic patient's lot requires a decision on his part; namely, he must decide to replace his compulsive and irrational suppression of the instincts with rational control. He need not capitulate to instinctual demands for complete and immediate happiness, but he must discontinue the practice of stifling legitimate requests for pleasure. In summary, the patient must allow reason (ego) to prevail as the mediator between his passions (id) and his harsh conscience (superego).

The Freudian method of correcting psychological disorder can be specified further by dividing attempted cures into two broad categories. The first comprises cases in which the psychoanalyst seeks the removal of superfluous inhibitions against the instincts; the second covers instances in which he promotes the imposition of needed restrictions. Naturally a particular case may involve a combination of these goals. Freud's own patients tended to be puritanical rather than libertine; hence most of them required therapy of the first sort. Various approaches can be used in encouraging a patient to lift inhibitions against his urges. In general, however, the strategy is to convince the patient that those inhibitions lack a rational foundation in that they hamper rather than help his interaction with the environment. For example, if a man suppresses his desire to sleep with his wife because of an inhibition against sex, then his resultant frustration presumably will detract from his performance as a loving father and stable provider. A Freudian would try to rectify the situation by first getting the patient to appreciate the irrationality of his inhibition, and he would hope eventually to bring the patient's feelings about sex into accord with the patient's own rational appraisal of its place in life.

Freudian psychotherapy now can be summarized. Such therapy aims at strengthening the position of reason (intellect) at the expense of both (1) the irrational demands of the instincts for absolute pleasure and (2) the overzealous disciplinary action that the self, through a harsh conscience, takes against its own instinctual desires. (The situations in which society at large imposes undue restrictions on the instincts will be discussed later.) The analyst tries to become an ally of the patient's ego (reason) in its endeavor to work out a rational compromise between the ambitions of the instincts and the exigencies of civilization survival. The therapy itself begins with an attempt to discover the particular urges or frustrations behind the patient's condition, and the process of discovery consists in the analysis (interpretation) of dreams and other data about the instincts. Once the analyst becomes reasonably sure of his diagnosis he tries to share his understanding of the patient's problem with the patient himself. A cure results if the patient makes a rational response to the condition he has come to understand.

The above summary indicated two crucial roles that reason or understanding plays in Freudian therapy. First, the interpretation of dreams and other clues about the instincts underlies the diagnosis (understanding) of a patient's disorder; hence reason has an *analytic* or *interpretative* function in practical psychoanalysis. Second, a cure requires that the patient himself bring his passions and his control over them into rational accord; hence reason also has a *regulatory* function in psychotherapy. The discussion that follows will concentrate on the regulatory function of reason. The key issue in this discussion can be stated in the form of a question: Can reason prevail in its battle against both the passions (id) and the forces that suppress them, especially the hyperactive superego? Freud's answer to this question determines the degree of his pessimism.

The Soft Voice of Reason

Freud's theory of instincts has inescapably pessimistic conclusions because it implies incompatibility between happiness and civilization-survival. Even the partial frustration of drives causes unhappiness because their slightest inhibition prevents the self from attaining a state of equilibrium, which Freud equates with perfect pleasure. Yet full satisfaction of drives (namely, the complete release of tension) coincides with death under the guise of Nirvana. The point can be summarized by saying that the theory of instincts supports a *general* pessimism about man's condition. Here we attempt to specify the degree of pessimism by considering the possible connections among the demands of the instincts, the self's repressive apparatus, and reason.

Freud's commentators usually agree that *The Future of an Illusion* contains the least pessimistic prognosis about man's becoming a truly rational animal. Such passages as the following furnish exegetic support for their position.

> We may insist as often as we like that man's intellect is powerless in comparison with his instinctual life, and we may be right in this. Nevertheless, there is something peculiar about this weakness. The voice of the intellect is a soft one, but it does not rest until it has gained a hearing. Finally, after a countless succession of rebuffs, it succeeds. This is one of the few points on which one may be optimistic about the future of mankind. But it is in itself a point of no small importance. And from it one can derive yet other hopes. The primacy of the intellect lies, it is true, in a distant, distant future, but probably not in an *infinitely* distant one. It presumably will set itself the same aims as those whose realization you expect from your God (of course within human limits—so far as external reality, Ananke, allows it), namely, the love of man and the decrease of suffering.[3]

These remarks might be construed as a retraction of the general pessimism in the theory of instincts. In order to avoid such a misinterpretation the quotation must be placed in context. Freud's tribute to reason falls within a polemic against religion. His guarded suggestion that reason may prevail someday should be read as an attack on religion, which Freud equates with superstition and illusion. The cautious prediction that the "primacy of the intellect" will become fact cannot be understood as a forecast that the strife between the instincts and the self's repressive apparatus can be overcome; man will have to endure unhappiness as long as the id and the superego remain locked in combat. Freud never promises that the rational conquest of religion will make man happy; instead, he offers the much more modest claim that the ascendancy of reason may decrease the level of unhappiness. In a passage shortly after the quotation above, Freud says as much.

> Education freed from the burden of religious doctrines will not, it may be, effect much change in man's psychological nature. Our god *logos* is perhaps not a very almighty one, and he may only be able to fulfill a small part of what his predecessors have promised.[4]

This short textual exploration has not been intended as a denial that Freud's writings vacillate between severe and almost mild pessimism. But even his least pessimistic remarks do not offset the sobering conclusions from the theory of instincts. Whenever Freud considers the role reason plays in determining man's condition he remembers to acknowledge that reason speaks with a soft voice; at any time it may be drowned out by the cacophonous cries of the instincts or by the superego's equally distracting clamor for their suppression. The remainder of this section will further specify the precarious position of reason.

In the present discussion the ego warrants attention primarily as the agency that injects rationality into behavior. The ego's chief function in this regard involves mediation of the relationship between the id and the superego; specifically, the Ego must permit gratification of the id's drives without allowing them to threaten the self's very existence. Complete repression of the instincts would deny the self any pleasure whatsoever, and life in these circumstances would be unbearable. Yet some repression must be maintained because the inalterable and uncompromising nature of the instincts makes them a constant threat to communal life and hence survival. The ego therefore must protect the self against either too much or too little domination of the id by the superego. Establishing such a balance in the first place is a difficult task; sustaining the balance creates a problem that lies at the basis of Freud's pessimism.

The ego has an especially difficult task because its past successes never guarantee a corresponding record in the future. An example again may be useful. Assume that a patient who has suffered from a harsh conscience eventually manages to end the superego's tyranny over the id. His improvement attests to the ability of his ego, under the psychotherapist's guidance, to assume a commanding position against both of the superego and the id. Yet the same problem may recur at any time, or a different one may arise in its stead. A brief glance at the theory of instincts provides the explanation. Since the id's ultimately self-destructive drives never vary at all, the need to control them remains throughout life. Thus the ego is always exposed to twin dangers. First, a relaxation in the superego's control over the id may lead to the irrational gratification of the instincts—irrational to the exact extent that it endangers survival. Second, an overindulgence in the superego's control of the id also may become irrational by denying the self even an amount of pleasure that poses no threat to survival.

Theoretical psychoanalysis, in summary, leaves open the possibility that the ego may forfeit at any time its dominant position within the self, assuming that the ego ever reaches such a position. Hence, practical psychoanalysis can promise no more than qualified success.[5] Freudian psychotherapy may be able to create or restore balance among the id, the ego, and the superego, but the balance will be lost if either the id or the superego manages to usurp the ego's very tenuous position. The threat that the other two agencies pose against the ego can be stated more economically and elegantly; the textual support comes from Freud's remark that Thanatos plays an especially villainous role in frustrating the efforts of both the psychotherapist and the patient's own ego. Thanatos threatens to undermine the rational compromise between instinctual gratification (id) and instinctual renunciation (superego), and in so doing works simultaneously against both happiness and survival. This line of inquiry will be pursued in the next section.

The Monism of the Death Instinct

One section in Chapter 6 was devoted to a discussion of a possible inconsistency in the theory of instincts. Freud's final dualism pits Life (Eros) against Death (Thanatos), but his account of pleasure, at least on the mechanistic model of the self, collapses the alleged distinction between the two primary instincts. In the mechanistic model pleasure consists in a diminution of tension. The id's desire for absolute pleasure therefore coincides with its quest for Nirvana, the state of completely tensionless existence. Since life vacillates between the production and reduction of tension, however, only death brings real equilibrium; hence the pursuit of unconditional pleasure constitutes a drive toward death. The theory of instincts articulates this conclusion with the principle that basic drives have a regressive tendency. The Death instinct in particular inclines the self toward the past because it seeks to restore the tensionless or inorganic state that precedes life. Thus the Death instinct's pursuit of absolute pleasure occurs as a regressive movement toward Nirvana, or inanimate existence.

The mechanistic conception of pleasure ingeniously equates death, absolute pleasure, Nirvana, perfect equilibrium, and preorganic existence. However, the equation seems to destroy Freud's desired dualism by merging the identities of Eros and Thanatos. The difficulty can be clarified with a short review of the Life instinct. Eros reportedly differs from Thanatos because Eros aims at the creation, instead of the destruction, of ever-expanding bonds among individuals. Under the guise of sexual passion and then affection, for instance, Eros promotes formation and, subsequently, preservation of the family. But if Eros qualifies as an instinct it must pursue absolute pleasure; and if such pleasure can be won only through Nirvana (death) the Life instinct ironically takes on the identity of the Death instinct.

As noted earlier, Freud tries to avoid this conclusion in two ways. First, he appeals to a rather bizarre myth in order to explain how Eros can display the regressive inclination that every instinct has without imitating the Death instinct's urge to restore the self's original state of inorganic (tensionless) existence. The myth, from Plato, suggests that the erotic impulse behind heterosexual intercourse represents an attempt to create anew the androgynous third sex, which antedated the two normal sexes. Freud eventually disavows this fanciful story.[6] His second effort to distinguish Eros from Thanatos involves a major revision in his theory about pleasure. Specifically, he tries to broaden the mechanistic model of the self so that pleasure no longer coincides with a diminution in tension. Freud's reasoning in the matter seems clear. If certain kinds of pleasure do not entail a movement toward death as the completely tensionless state, then an instinct—namely, an automatic and irrational drive for pleasure—other than Thanatos can exist.

Thus Freud attempts to salvage the distinction between Eros and Thanatos by delimiting (a) pleasure as a reduction in tension from (b) pleasure as some sort of erotic satisfaction. Unfortunately, however, he offers no satisfactory explanation of (b); he rests his case on rather vague intimations about a type of pleasure that does not involve the quest for Nirvana. Further, the distinction between (a) and (b) threatens to betray the central insight in the theory of instincts. Part of Freud's appeal as a theoretician lies in his ability to present a systematic or unifying account of ostensibly divergent phenomena. The most obvious example is the way he furnishes a uniform explanation for every kind of pleasure, ranging from orgasm to contemplation of art: pleasure always results from a reduction in tension, and it increases in amount as the reduced tension approaches the ideal of Nirvana (death). Once pleasure has been separated into two categories, however, the theory of instincts loses elegance, explanatory force, and perhaps even consistency. To draw a distinction between (a) and (b) amounts to conceding that pleasure lacks a single origin and nature; yet the conviction that all kinds of pleasure are fundamentally the same lies at the very foundation of psychoanalysis.

The difficulty here can be summarized this way. Freud's division of pleasure into two categories apparently detracts rather than adds to the theory of instincts and may even generate an inconsistency in the theory. This criticism can be expressed in a more positive fashion. The theory of instincts can function perfectly well with a single category of pleasure and therefore with a single primary instinct. Since the distinction between (a) and (b) corresponds to the difference between Thanatos and Eros, respectively, a unification of the two primal instincts would automatically collapse the distinction between the two kinds of pleasure. The argument in the remainder of this section favors a single primary instinct, Thanatos. A cautionary note seems appropriate at the outset. The discussion will strain the customs of textual examination by appealing only to carefully selected passages in Freud's work. This procedure must be followed in order to specify those implications in the theory of instincts that Freud himself seems unwilling to accept. Thus the purpose here is not to recapitulate Freud's remarks with scrupulous accuracy but, rather, to indicate the thrust of his theory.

The test to determine whether Freudian theory remains intact without Eros consists in using Thanatos alone to carry the explanatory load that formerly fell on both of the primary instincts. The argument that Thanatos by itself proves adequate to the task will center on three topics: (1) the unending clash between the instincts and the requirements of civilization-survival; (2) the notion of sublimation; (3) the growth of anxiety and guilt as an index of social evolution.

The theory of instincts gives special emphasis to the truism about man's being a social animal by making communal life into a precondition for personal survival. Normally an isolated individual has no chance of holding his own against the environment—an obvious fact that implies the unavoidability of membership in a group. Freudian theory accounts for the fact by closely linking the requirements for civilization with those for personal survival. These requirements can be condensed into a single and appropriately general one; namely, man must deny himself pleasure in the interest of civilization-survival. The requirement arises because man must divide a limited amount of energy between his own quest for pleasure and the demands of civilization-survival (for instance, work).

The phenomenon under discussion can be characterized as

the "inevitable clash between the instincts and civilization." The dualistic theory of instincts explains the clash partially with reference to the divergent inclinations of Eros and Thanatos. The Life instinct works *for* civilization because it aims at establishing harmonious relationships among individuals; hence it deters the individual from pursuing pleasure on a merely egoistic basis. The Death instinct, however, moves in an antisocial direction because it impels each individual to abandon the responsibilities of civilization-survival in favor of Nirvana, the state of perfect quietude or inaction. Thus Eros serves civilization by uniting individuals into groups, while Thanatos undermines it by driving them apart.

This apparently clear opposition between the two primary drives becomes obscure on inspection. Eros sometimes works *against* civilization-survival. A case in point is the sexual attachment that becomes so strong that it interferes with socially necessary work and so has the effect of placing a purely individual gain in pleasure above the requirements of civilization-survival. Thanatos, in turn, often helps rather than hinders social life. For example, it furnishes the energy behind man's conquest of nature. The supposed boundary between the two instincts can be disputed on other grounds as well. For instance, Eros has a key role in sexual relationships because it promotes the harmonious unification of individuals, yet Thanatos also shares in the formation of such relationships because it pursues orgasm, or drastic reduction in sexual tension, as an approximation of Nirvana.

This discussion has tried to indicate how the two primary instincts converge in certain respects. If Eros and Thanatos cannot be sharply distinguished from each other, then the suspicion grows that they may not be distinct. It remains to show, however, that Thanatos alone can assume all instinctual functions.

An earlier remark that the Life instinct aids civilization by bringing individuals together into harmonious groups must be qualified, even on a dualistic reading of psychoanalysis. Only *sublimated* Eros contributes to civilization-survival. This conclusion follows from the axiom that an instinct has absolute pleasure as its goal, and such pleasure remains incompatible with civilization-survival. Instinctual energy therefore must be deflected or diverted from its original aim in order to serve socially useful purposes, and the deflection constitutes sublimation.

The contrast between sublimated and unsublimated Eros can be illustrated with the previously used example of a sexual attachment that interferes with socially necessary work; only after Eros has been properly controlled can it help society by encouraging cohesive unions such as the family. That unsublimated Eros threatens civilization, however, weakens the putative distinction between the two primary instincts, for Eros no longer can be distinguished from Thanatos on the grounds that Eros tends to support civilization while Thanatos tends to undermine it. The disruption of civilization can occur whenever instinctual energy lacks control (sublimation), regardless of whether the energy flows from Eros or Thanatos. Thus the distinction between sublimated and unsublimated instinctual energy, rather than the disputable demarcation of Eros from Thanatos, explains the ambivalent relation between the instincts and civilization-survival.

Details now can be added to the general thesis that the theory of instincts needs only Thanatos. A monism of the Death instinct accounts for the familiar antagonism between the individual and the group (society). Under the sway of Thanatos the individual automatically pursues unconditional pleasure in the form of Nirvana (death). This course of action is blatantly selfish and antisocial because an individual can reach a state of perfect pleasure only by renouncing the basic social obligation to place the interests of the group above his own desires. In more prosaic terms, the search for complete tranquility or Nirvana diverts energy from such socially necessary activities as work.

The relationships among Thanatos, sublimation, and civilization-survival extend even further. Sublimation of the Death instinct does more than ensure the mere possibility of civilization-survival;

it furnishes the energy that actually creates, sustains, and expands communal life. The point becomes clear in light of what happens to the sublimated energy from Thanatos. Instead of supporting the individually and socially destructive pursuit of Nirvana, such energy contributes to increased (a) self-control and (b) security. Effect (a) will be considered shortly; (b) refers to the various ways in which a society secures its position through, for example, conquest of the environment. Thus sublimated Thanatos has one of the beneficent results that Freud attributes to Eros; namely, the sublimated Death instinct provides energy for the construction, preservation, and expansion of civilization.

A second similarity between sublimated Thanatos and the supposed Life instinct deserves consideration. The reasoning behind Freud's belief in a primordial Life instinct can be recapitulated this way. There must be an instinct that counters the self-destructive, antisocial thrust of Thanatos; otherwise the Death instinct's drive for completely selfish pleasure in the form of Nirvana would be successful. Eros therefore seems necessary to explain the affinity among individuals that underlies civilization; since man can survive only as a group member, the Life instinct furnishes the energy that permits and promotes survival. Thus Eros and Thanatos stand in diametric opposition because Eros draws people together in the interests of life while Thanatos drives them apart through an egoistic preoccupation with Nirvana (death). The contrast between the two instincts can be made even sharper by recalling that Thanatos also goes under the name *Destructive instinct*; as the agent of destruction, Thanatos threatens to disintegrate the harmonious bonds among individuals that must be preserved to allow the species to endure.

The main point here is that the tension between man's antisocial and prosocial tendencies can be explained solely with reference to the difference between unsublimated and sublimated Thanatos; the distinction between Eros and Thanatos appears superfluous in this regard. This claim can be defended with a short review of what sublimation accomplishes in Thanatos. Sublimated energy from the Death instinct moves either inwardly or outwardly. If such energy flows away from the self its destructive potential still can be used to either the benefit or the detriment of civilization-survival. For example, the agricultural conquest of nature usually aids society while war often threatens it, and both activities draw on Thanatos for energy. An inward movement of this energy reinforces the superego, whose chief function involves control of the instincts; hence inwardly deflected energy from Thanatos ironically promotes further disciplinary action against it. The superego can perform additional services for civilization-survival as it gains strength from its inward diversion or sublimation of energy from the Death instinct. This point should not be surprising. Since the superego acts as society's ambassador within the self, it naturally encourages behavior that aids society against the egoistic or antisocial quest for Nirvana. The inward sublimation of Thanatos therefore accomplishes the very feat that an instinctual dualism attributes to Eros; that is, it supplies energy for the construction and preservation of civilization.

The purpose of this discussion has been to illustrate that the inwardly sublimated Death instinct can take over a key function of Eros. By strengthening the superego, which acts on behalf of society as a whole against the purely selfish quest for Nirvana, an inward sublimation of Thanatos assimilates each person into society; hence the process has the effect of unifying individuals. If only inwardly sublimated Thanatos binds people together, though, the resultant unions should lack the harmonious and even pleasurable quality that presumably would be present if an erotic instinct accoumplished the task.

The difference can be specified further by reviewing the nature of both instincts in their unsublimated condition. Even apart from sublimation the Life instinct aims at the unification of individuals; thus sublimation affects only the intensity rather than the direction of its basic thrust. Sublimated Eros merely substitutes bonds of affection for those of passion. The unsublimated Death instinct, conversely, has intrinsically divisive effects because it impels the purely egoistic pursuit of Nirvana; hence sublimation *reverses* the bent of the Death instinct by diverting its energy from destruction toward construction and preservation of society. Sublimation resembles outright frustration in Thanatos, but it has the appearance of simple control or discipline in Eros. The difference in question implies that civilization founded exclusively on the inward sublimation of Thanatos forfeits much happiness just because the Death instinct pursues *intrinsically* antisocial pleasure—Nirvana. The point also can be made with reference to the notions of guilt and anxiety.

The inward flow of energy from the Death instinct fortifies the superego, the agency that bears primary responsibility for guilt. In a familiar example, the superego sometimes punishes the self with pangs of conscience. Since the superego draws on the Death instinct for energy, guilt may be characterized as punishment that Thanatos, operating under the superego's supervision, inflicts on the self. Various factors can generate feelings of guilt; in general, however, the condition arises either after the self gratifies a desire that the superego finds objectionable or, in extreme cases, after the self merely entertains such a desire.

Guilt also can be described as a severe reaction against the self's efforts to overcome anxiety, another condition that betrays the presence of the superego in that it stems from the superego's excessive interdiction against pleasure. Tension results from this injunction because the desire for pleasure, or tensionless existence, never abates; the timeless id does not alter its demand for absolute pleasure even after the demand has been repeatedly refused. The state of frustration that attends the superego's harsh action against the id can be equated with anxiety. Thus the superego condemns the self to fluctuate between the equally unenviable poles of guilt and anxiety; namely, the superego produces anxiety by its refusal to honor enough of the id's demands, and it generates guilt when the ego sides with the id by granting demands for pleasure that the superego finds objectionable. Finally, the superego relies on energy specifically from the Death instinct, which has ironic implications because suppression of Thanatos causes anxiety and its gratification precipitates guilt.

The preceding interpretation of psychoanalysis as an instinctual monism cannot escape the conclusion that a society erected solely on the sublimation of Thanatos will be afflicted with anxiety and guilt. Significantly, Freud's later writings acknowledge that modern civilization seems condemned to this condition—a conclusion for which evidence is readily available. As man assumes the indisputably dominant position in nature, for instance, his own destructive impulses become the greatest threat to his survival. The point has been emphasized in the many sobering truisms about man's possessing the nuclear machinery to eradicate himself. Aggression in the form of nuclear war would constitute one manifestation of Thanatos, the Destructive instinct. The best way to preclude such a manifestation consists in giving the energy from Thanatos an inward direction. Two considerations dictate this choice. First, the inward sublimation of Thanatos reinforces the superego, which, in turn, acts to control the socially destructive impulses of Thanatos. Second, even if the inward sublimation of Thanatos proves excessive, at least the individual rather than civilization as a whole suffers the resulting aggression.

Apparently the inward sublimation of Thanatos must continue as long as civilization maintains the technological potential to destroy itself, for, to repeat this crucial thesis of psychoanalysis, the destructive bent of Thanatos never changes. The sole alternative to strengthening the superego through the inward deflection of Thanatos would seem to involve some artificial means of controlling the instinct. The means might range from tranquilizer to lobotomy; yet use of such means would leave civilization more secure from the threat of the Destructive instinct without making civilized man any happier. Genuine pleasure accompanies only the *gratification* of urges, and the use of sophisticated pharmaceutical or surgical devices to deter the Destructive instinct would subdue its urges rather than fulfill them. At best these devices would substitute a semblance of instinctual fulfillment for the real thing.

A related topic deserves mention here. As the technological potential for destruction advances, society's ability to control its members evidently shows comparable gains. Even at present, for example, the lobotomy and other extreme measures hardly exhaust the techniques society has at its disposal for influencing behavior; alternative devices range from crude brainwashing to subliminal propaganda. Thus civilization has acquired the means for regulating the instincts as the need for such regulation has grown more acute; specifically, society has developed very sophisticated ways of training the individual to discipline his own id. This increased control amounts to enhancing the authority the superego exercises over the instincts. If the superego continues to gain strength at the expense of instinctual satisfaction, however, anxiety and guilt also should increase, for the first condition arises from the frustration of any drive, and the second stems from fortification of the superego with energy taken specifically from Thanatos. A rise in anxiety and guilt may provide an index of social evolution; hence future civilization may demand an ever greater sacrifice in happiness as the price of security.

Freud's later works, such as *Civilization and Its Discontents*, paint the same bleak picture as the instinctual monism outlined here. Nevertheless, he never abandons the theory of two primary instincts, which brings up again the question about the purpose of the preceding discussion. That question can be answered in three parts.

First, Freudian theory owes part of its strength to the insight that seemingly diverse kinds of pleasure have a common origin and character; namely, every pleasure results from the satisfaction of a drive, and every pleasure constitutes a reduction in the tension caused by the frustration of a drive. The introduction of Eros compromises this insight because the instinct reportedly pursues a kind of pleasure that does not have Nirvana, or completely tensionless existence, as its ideal. A monism of the Death instinct therefore seems more faithful to a basic principle in psychoanalysis than does the dualism of Eros and Thanatos.

Second, the dualistic theory apparently suffers from inconsistency because Eros does not fit the definition of an instinct as an urge "to restore an earlier state of things"; Thanatos, however, exemplifies a regressive inclination because it aims at restoring the state of inorganic existence that precedes life itself. Third, Freud acknowledges throughout the mature theory of instincts that Thanatos poses the main difficulty for both psychotherapy on an individual basis and civilization-survival as such. The monistic theory lends emphasis to the problematical character of Thanatos by making it the sole primary instinct.[7]

A final point seems in order. Freud's dualistic theory of instincts remains less pessimistic than the monistic version by offering the vague forecast that Eros and erotic pleasure may continue to prevent a disastrous release of energy from Thanatos. However, the forecast cannot be read as a guarantee that the Life instinct always will enjoy victory in its ongoing struggle with the Death instinct.

This section has considered the most pessimistic elements in Freudian theory. Alternative readings inject Freudianism with an optimistic and sometimes utopian tone. Let us consider one of these interpretations.

Marcuse's Utopian Reading of Freud

The preceding sections have traced the thread of pessimism that runs directly from theoretical to practical psychoanalysis. The theory of instincts teaches that psychotherapy never will devise a final cure for the discontent (*Unbehagen*) that afflicts civilization, for this condition reflects the irresolvable clash between the demands of the instincts, especially Thanatos, and the exigencies of civilization-survival. Attempts have been made to circumvent the somber conclusions of psychoanalytic theory by viewing the conflict between happiness and survival as historically determinate and therefore merely transitory. Marcuse's attempt warrants special consideration because it draws so liberally from Freud's own insights. Although Marcuse's thought deserves attention in its own right, this discussion is confined to the way he invests Freudianism with a utopian content. By examining the principles Marcuse must amend in order to devest Freudian theory of its pessimism, this discussion should further clarify the limits of practical psychoanalysis.

Marcuse's major work on Freud, *Eros and Civilization*, aims at restoring to a position of prominence the critical theme in psychoanalysis, its "hidden trend." This theme can be easily missed because Freud's conception of man contains both ". . . the most irrefutable indictment of Western civilization—and at the same time the most unshakable defense of this civilization."[8] Marcuse contends that the critical face of psychoanalysis has been obscured by those therapists who counsel the patient to adjust to the current social order—advice that ignores the possibility that society must be radically changed before the patient can be cured. In different terms, Marcuse accuses practical psychoanalysis of harboring conservative predilections because it usually sides with civilization against the individual. The psychotherapist exemplifies this conservatism when he encourages a patient to acquiesce in society's demands instead of rebelling against them; hence psychotherapy acts, perhaps only inadvertently, on behalf of the establishment whenever it advises the patient to accept his place in the system. Finally, Marcuse condemns the conservatism of practical psychoanalysis on the grounds that modern industrial society oppresses the individual; for him the appropriate response to the patient's condition may involve a drastic change in civilization.

In formulating his critique of advanced industrial society Marcuse looks to psychoanalytic theory because it ". . . penetrates the protective ideology in so far as it views the cultural institutions in terms of what they have made of the individuals through whom they function."[9] The quotation alludes to the notions through which

Freudianism reduces cultural phenomena to the tension between happiness and survival. Just one example is Freud's account of sublimation, which places civilization—the vehicle of survival—on a foundation of denied pleasure. The account stresses that energy can be allocated to civilization only by diverting it from the pursuit of absolute pleasure. Thus psychoanalysis becomes a critique of civilization in pointing out the price in individual happiness that must be paid for the benefits of communal life. Psychoanalysis has a debunking effect on any ideology that sides unconditionally with society against the individual. Consider Marcuse's endeavor to sharpen the critical tools he finds in Freud.

Marcuse expands Freud's analysis of sublimation by distinguishing between (a) repressive desublimation and (b) nonrepressive sublimation. The distinction appears problematical from the perspective of orthodox psychoanalysis. Since sublimation prevents the full and immediate gratification of urges, it seems intrinsically repressive; since desublimation removes restraints against such gratification, it seems necessarily nonrepressive. Marcuse acknowledges the apparent inconsistency between the original notion of sublimation and his two amendments, but he justifies categories (a) and (b) by showing that their introduction into psychoanalysis enables it to offer a more sophisticated explanation of advanced industrial society. The two categories will be considered in order.

The category of repressive desublimation covers the ingenious ways society manipulates sexuality as an instrument of oppression. This manipulation has an ironic quality because the release or desublimation of the instincts normally favors the individual's demands for pleasure at the expense of society's dictates and expectations. In an obvious illustration of (a), Marcuse cites the use of sex in business.

> It has often been noted that advanced industrial civilization operates with a greater degree of sexual freedom— "operates" in the sense that the latter becomes a market value and a factor of social mores. Without ceasing to be an instrument of labor, the body is allowed to exhibit its

sexual features in the everyday work world and in work relations. This is one of the unique achievements of industrial society—rendered possible by the reduction of dirty and heavy physical labor; by the availability of cheap, attractive clothing, beauty culture, and physical hygiene; by the requirements of the advertising industry, etc. The sexy office and sales girls, the handsome, virile junior executive and floor walker are highly marketable commodities, and the possession of suitable mistresses—once the prerogative of kings, princes, and lords—facilitates the career of even the less exalted ranks in the business community.[10]

Repressive desublimation defuses the instincts so that they no longer endanger society. Simply to confine instinctual energy would be to increase the danger of its sudden release, leading to disruption or even upheaval of the system. Further, such desublimation wins the citizenry's loyalty by injecting sexuality into everyday life; people begin to assume that a different kind of society would have to be less enjoyable. Thus repressive desublimation has the effect of pacifying individuals so that their quest for pleasure poses no threat of revolution against the established order. Marcuse condemns (a) precisely because it nullifies the revolutionary potential of the instincts, for he insists that to destroy contemporary society and replace it with an industrial system void of competitive economics would augment gratification of the instincts. In summary, Marcuse views repressive desublimation as oppression by means of distraction and delusion. Because such oppression promotes the misconception that life under the current industrial system cannot be improved, (a) tends to dissuade citizens from seeking the system's overthrow.

The category of nonrepressive sublimation shares the critical function of (a) and also contains the key to Marcuse's utopian reading of Freud. Marcuse uses (b) as part of his argument that subjugation of the instincts can be inevitable without being irreversible. His point can be clarified.

Both Marcuse and Freud agree on the necessity of civilization for man's survival, and they concur that civilization must begin with repression of the instincts. Their disagreement arises over the issue of whether such repression constitutes a *permanent* precondition for civilization-survival. Marcuse breaks with orthodox Freudianism by insisting that much repression of the instincts becomes unnecessary and obsolete after the problem of abundance has been solved; at that moment in history the previous repression of the instincts should be reversed. Thus Marcuse insists that an affluent society like contemporary America can afford to encourage nonrepressive sublimation of the instincts. The difference between the two positions can be expressed in different terms. Only Marcuse treats subjugation of the instincts as a historical phenomenon that can disappear in an era of abundance. Freud's reasons for rejecting this optimistic thesis will be considered later; first, however, Marcuse's critique of the contemporary industrial order should be stated with more precision.

The current system allegedly perpetuates itself through its enforcement of "surplus repression." Such repression must be distinguished from "basic repression," or the amount of control over the instincts that must be maintained for civilized survival. Since civilization-survival does not require *surplus* repression, its sole rationale lies in perpetuation of oppressive institutions and practices. (That American businessmen still must dress in a certain way provides a minor illustration of surplus repression.) If a society unnecessarily retards satisfaction of drives, though, it stands guilty of imposing irrational restraints on pleasure. Marcuse's main objection against the modern industrial system concerns its dispensable and therefore intolerable denial of happiness.

Marcuse makes an additional refinement in Freudian theory. The presence of surplus repression reflects that the "performance principle" governs life under the present industrial system. This principle is the version of Freud's reality principle that prevails today in industrial society. The matter can be explained as follows. According to both Marcuse and Freud, the self cannot survive so long as the instincts remain under the "pure" or "unrestrained" pleasure principle, because this principle allows full and immediate gratification of drives, which amounts to death under the guise of Nirvana. The reality principle, conversely, permits only the partial and delayed fulfillment of drives; hence it offers a compromise between pleasure and survival. Marcuse complains that the current industrial system has transformed the reality principle into the performance principle by making economic competition into a precondition for survival. On the grounds that industrial society now has amassed sufficient wealth to dispense with fierce economic competition among individuals, Marcuse concludes that life under the performance principle results in surplus repression; for if this principle causes sacrifices in pleasure that are not strictly necessary for survival, then it automatically takes an excessive toll in happiness.

The notion of nonrepressive sublimation can be defined partially in terms of surplus repression and the performance principle. This kind of sublimation presupposes the elimination of surplus repression, which in the present industrial system can be ended only by replacing the performance principle with a more rational version of the reality principle. Yet the mere absence of surplus repression does not coincide with nonrepressive sublimation or (b). At the outset of civilization, for example, repressive control of the instincts was necessary for survival and so could not be construed as excessive. Nonrepressive sublimation distinguishes itself from every other instance of restraint on the instincts because (b) actually generates pleasure; sublimation normally entails a loss of pleasure because it decreases gratification of the instincts.

Marcuse does not confine his explication of (b) to abstract descriptions; he offers as an example of nonrepressive sublimation esthetic experience, which resembles such unpleasant kinds of sublimation as work because both involve the *controlled* release of instinctual energy. Esthetic experience also seems intrinsically enjoyable, however. For one, art has a cathartic function so that it can bring about the tension reduction that psychoanalysis equates with pleasure. Moreover, artistic activity (in the creation or the enjoyment of art) appears closer to play than to work because it includes the element of fun. Esthetic experience thus uniquely combines sublimation and instinctual gratification; hence it deflects energy away from the pursuit of absolute pleasure in such a way that the deflection itself—namely, the act of producing or enjoying a work of art—gives compensatory pleasure.

Additional details in Marcuse's analysis of nonrepressive sublimation will not be needed here. It suffices to mention that his alternative to the current industrial system consists in a society that maintains a high level of technology and wealth but at the same time substitutes esthetic for purely economic considerations. In brief, Marcuse's vision of an industrial utopia draws on suggestions from Marx. The main point here, however, concerns the extent to which orthodox Freudianism can accommodate Marcuse's views.

The notions of surplus repression and the performance principle pose little difficulty in this regard. Although Freud insists that civilization remains impossible apart from repression of the instincts, he acknowledges that society can be too repressive. His efforts as a therapist to allevaite the guilt that many of his patients contracted from their Victorian environment demonstrates his opposition to surplus repression. In addition, Freud hardly approves of every variation of the reality principle; hence he would have no qualms about condemning a principle of economic competitiveness that leads to surplus repression. The question whether the concept of nonrepressive sublimation can be incorporated into the original Freudian position does not have such an easy answer; the response depends on the emphasis given to the adjective *nonrepressive*. Marcuse himself points out the writings in which Freud seems to admit that artistic and related activities involve a kind of sublimation that lacks the clearly repressive character of, say, work,[11] but the admission does not undermine the principle that sublimation of an instinct always entails a deprivation of pleasure. To say that the sublimation of an urge equals its frustration is not to deny that notably different degrees of both may exist. Thus artistic activity may be pleasurable in comparison with manual labor; nevertheless, the implication is only that artistic activity involves *less* repression than does manual labor. The same matter can be expressed differently. Freud grants in principle that different kinds of sublimation cannot be equally deleterious; otherwise his endeavors to cure a patient of excessive self-repression would be futile and perhaps even cynical. The question arises, however, whether even the most preferable (that is, the least repressive) kind of sublimation can match the pleasure that would result in its absence. Freud's response to this query is a resounding No!—an answer that affirms the repressive character of all sublimation.

The notion of nonrepressive sublimation must be understood as less repressive sublimation in order to find a place in orthodox psychoanalysis. The essential difference between Marcuse and Freud can be expressed in less technical and more emphatic terms. Both thinkers belong to the industrial age; yet they have different attitudes about the benefits of industrialization. Marcuse sees prospects for liberating the instincts in the technological conquest of nature because he identifies scarcity or want as the paramount cause of their repression. Marcuse therefore envisions an era of happiness in the wake of abundance. Freud, despite his acknowledgement of the industrial miracle, sees little hope for emancipation of the instincts. He stresses the ambivalent character of advancing technology, which, besides enhancing man's security, also furnishes the Destructive instinct with more dangerous instruments of expression. Of course, Marcuse recognizes the destructive potential of technology, but he anticipates a state of affairs in which instinctual aggression wanes as instinctual liberation increases. Freud, conversely, remains faithful to the principle that the primary instincts *never* change their basic thrust; so the only way to curb the Destructive instinct is to sublimate it—a process that condemns civilized man to a life of endless anxiety, guilt, and fear of self-annihilation. Marcuse expresses with precision this difference in attitude.

If sexuality is in its very essence anti-social and asocial, and if destructiveness is the manifestation of a primary instinct, then the idea of a nonrepressive reality principle would be nothing but idle speculation.[12]

Pessimism and Progress

Objections against Freudian theory will be discussed in Chapter 8, but one seems especially relevant at present. The criticism condemns psychoanalysis for having undesirable implications, a charge that specifically concerns the pessimistic doctrine that the struggle between man's desire for absolute pleasure and his need for civilization never will reach a happy conclusion.[13] The doctrine apparently implies the futility of trying to improve the human condition through education, psychotherapy, political action, and other means. In such a light Freud appears to preach the gospel of resignation and perhaps despair. His position can be seen in an even more unfavorable light. If civilized life requires that an individual renounce his ambition for purely egoistic pleasure (particularly in the form of Nirvana), and if psychoanalysis insists on the necessity of the sacrifice, then this theory apparently condones social regimentation. In stronger language, Freudian theory seems to ally itself with totalitarian politics by stressing the extent to which an individual's desires must bow to the interests of the group.

The issue of whether psychoanalysis advocates resignation and conformism can be settled only through careful inspection of its pessimism. That the theory seeks to demarcate the limits of instinctual liberation hardly means that it disclaims every attempt to increase happiness, and just because the theory affirms the incompatibility between civilization-survival and perfect pleasure does not imply that it sides unconditionally with society against the individual. Confusion on such matters results from the blurring of fine but essential distinctions. The sense in which the requirements of civilization take precedence over the wishes of the individual illustrate the point. By defending the social need to discipline the instincts, Freud takes a stand against the individual's desire to gratify them completely; yet Freud does so *solely* on the grounds that preservation of the race through civilization presupposes the renunciation of absolute pleasure. Freud himself emphasizes that repression of the instincts warrants condemnation once it ceases to be a precondition for survival. In summary, psychoanalysis resists those simplistic interpretations that place it at one extreme just because it does not lie at the other. Freud's warning against full emancipation of the instincts implies no commitment to their total repression.

Although psychoanalysis does not deal explicitly with the issue of political action, the theory's implications in this regard seem clear enough. Freud's scepticism about any promise to eliminate unhappiness by reconstructing society reflects the principle that any kind of civilization requires some repression of drives and therefore some unhappiness. His reservations about utopian politics, though, should not be construed as a plea against having aspirations; his pessimism merely cautions that plans for improving man's lot ought to be written in realism. Psychoanalysis condones neither reactionary programs nor political inaction, but it likewise condemns the attractive yet facile supposition that every problem has its solution.

Freud's position can be summarized with the dictum that even the best effects of future political action will fall within *presently* specifiable boundaries; namely, such action may lead to a marked reduction in suffering and unhappiness, but it cannot cause these phenomena to disappear altogether. The importance of this cautionary note, which seems almost too trite for attention, perhaps becomes evident only with reference to political activity that contravenes it. In the present century, for example, much bloodletting has been justified with utopian promises.[14] Even pretended belief in such promises is dangerous because it permits the myth of earthly bliss to gain a position of respectability; and the myth cannot be dismissed as harmless if it lends any support whatsoever to political ventures that never can compensate for the misery that results from them. Nazism is but one example of such a venture.

The aim of this brief section has been to offer a provisional defense of psychoanalysis against the charge that its pessimism implies the worthlessness of every attempt to improve man's condition. The discussion also touched on a topic that will receive more consideration in Chapter 8: how psychoanalysis acts as a critique of utopian politics. In closing it may be worthwhile to let Freud outline his own position on the role political and other activity should play in liberating the instincts from undue repression.

> Neurosis does not deny the existence of reality, it merely tries to ignore it; psychosis denies it and tries to substitute something else for it. A reaction which combines features of both of these is the one which we call normal or ''healthy''; it denies reality as little as neurosis, but then, like psychosis, it is concerned with effecting a change in reality. This expedient normal attitude leads naturally to some achievement in the outer world and is not content, like a psychosis, with establishing the alteration within itself.[15]

8
Antiutopianism
and
Progress

Freud's Moderate Pessimism

Psychoanalysis combines simplicity with erudition. Its central insight can be expressed with the platitude that man must divide his energy between the struggle for survival and the pursuit of pleasure—a division that generates conflict and frustration. The self's ambitions for perfect happiness can be fulfilled only by indulging the egoistic bent of the instincts, and such indulgence necessarily leads to death under the guise of Nirvana. The price for life therefore remains the instinctual frustration that underlies civilization. Of course, society tries to compensate the individual for his loss of pleasure with security and other substitutes, such as religion; the instincts, however, never relent in their demand for full and immediate gratification. Around this insight Freud builds a system in which almost every facet of civilization has its place.

The temptation to interpret psychoanalysis as thoroughly pessimistic has been discussed. Nevertheless, it may be instructive to recall how Freud tempers his pessimism without falling into romanticism. His antiutopian stand on the issue of unhappiness rests on the conviction that no improvement in man's surroundings, physical or social, can eliminate the need to deflect energy away from satisfaction of the instincts. This deflection will always constitute a precondition for civilization and therefore survival itself. If unconditional pleasure precludes survival, however, then even the future limits of happiness can be specified at present; namely, happiness always will be less than perfect because unhappiness remains its inseparable partner.

This conclusion seems trite only apart from a contrast with the utopian alternative, which affirms at least the possibility of complete happiness; further, the importance of the conclusion should become clearer through reflection on its practical ramifications. The point must be repeated here, however, that the mixture of happiness and unhappiness may comprise significantly different proportions of each ingredient. Freud's own efforts at psychotherapy reflect his belief that the Victorian age, for instance, did not allow enough instinctual satisfaction—hence his clinical work aimed at increasing happiness at the expense of undue repression.

Perhaps the best way to illustrate Freud's modified pessimism is to consider an analogous case from the history of ideas. In the *Critique of Pure Reason* Kant proposes to indicate the borders within which the search for knowledge must be confined. His demarcation separates the realm of possible (sensory) experience from the reality that presumably lies beyond it. Any trespass into the nonperceptual world ensures only confusion between knowledge and illusion; hence putative knowledge about God, for example, must be dismissed as illusory because God cannot be an object of perceptual experience. Kant's dictum that genuine knowledge extends to perceptually accessible objects alone restricts science, as a body of demonstrably true statements about reality, in the sense that the dictum forbids scientific expeditions into the transperceptual world. Yet the dictum neither denies nor discourages the continued growth of science. On the contrary, the warning that the limits of knowledge coincide with the boundaries of possible perceptual experience aids science by directing the quest for knowledge toward goals that can be reached, thereby discouraging the waste of energy on insoluble disputes over God, the soul, and other transperceptual matters. Kant therefore maintains that his proposed restrictions on the pursuit of knowledge will expedite its acquisition.[1]

Freud's stand against utopianism can be viewed in a similar light. His doctrine that life cannot support absolute happiness does not condone man's present lot by condemning every attempt at progress but, rather, provides an appraisal of the prospects for happiness so that efforts to improve the human condition will not be squandered on utopian schemes.

Freudian theory cannot be dismissed on the grounds that it counsels resignation as the proper response to unhappiness. That the theory supports only a moderate pessimism, though, does not establish its credibility; it may be rejected for some other reason. The point can be stated with greater precision. Psychoanalysis qualifies as a palatable and perhaps even convenient assumption for action because the theory acknowledges the possibility of a better future; any theory that denies this possibility discourages the effort to improve man's situation. Yet psychoanalysis may be appealing as an inspiration or a justification for action without being true, just as Marxism may promote revolution despite its inadequate (and in this sense false) account of man. In simple terms, the appeal that psychoanalysis may have as a basis for action does not establish its truth. Let us consider now the question of whether Freudian theory can be verified at all.

Psychoanalysis and Verification

Verification of any theory poses difficulties that on inspection appear almost insurmountable. Even within an established science, such as physics or chemistry, the choice of one theory over others usually cannot be justified on the basis of verification, because supporting data generally can be found for each competitor. Evidence rarely favors one theory so decisively that "demonstrably true" (verified) or "demonstrably false" (falsified) can be used to demarcate it from its rivals.

The problem of adducing enough evidence to either verify or falsify a theory has many facets. For one, evidence never occurs in a pristine state; hence competing theorists cannot find "pure evidence," "uninterpreted data," or "naked facts" to act as arbiter in deciding which position should be recognized as the true one. Evidence gathering in support of a theory requires selectivity. Otherwise it would be impossible to eliminate from consideration the data that have no bearing at all on the theory, and the collection of irrelevant data would hamper the task of verification. But the selective accumulation of data becomes prejudicial once it begins to screen out undesired evidence. A simple example can be used to illustrate the problem. Ptolemaic astronomers, who regarded the solar system as geocentric, sought to verify their ingenious hypotheses about astral and planetary motion by appealing to observation. Yet to select the observed or apparent movement of the stars and the sun as evidence in support of Ptolemaic astronomy strengthens the erroneous belief that these bodies move while the earth remains stationary. Such a selection of data invites the criticism that precisely the wrong evidence has received the most attention. Thus the data that *confirm* a theory may be insufficient to *verify* it, which suggests that amassing evidence in support of a theory does not constitute its verification.[2]

The attempt to verify psychoanalysis may appear futile in light of the problems that arise even in such a field as astronomy.[3] The truth of Freudian theory cannot be established merely by listing the ways in which the data of both history and present experience confirm its tenets; comparable evidence against these tenets also can be supplied. In addition, psychoanalysis contains predictions (for instance, it forecasts a perpetual antagonism between the instincts and civilization), and claims about the future obviously cannot be verified in the present. These and related difficulties suggest that it may be misguided to expect an indisputable verification of psychoanalysis. Accordingly, the remainder of this section contains a review of some matters on which psychoanalysis seems clearly in accord with significant data. Instead of an attempt to verify the theory, however, the review is confined to the more modest task of advertising points that recommend the theory for serious consideration.

Psychoanalysis cuts through euphemisms about civilized life by linking civilization with the loss of happiness. The theory thus furnishes a perspective from which the ambivalence of civilization appears striking. On the positive side civilization acts as the guarantor of survival, because the community usually can protect itself better than the isolated individual can protect himself. Civilization also serves as the guardian of past accomplishments as it transmits a heritage of technology, law, art, religion from one generation to the next, thereby promoting continued contributions to the legacy. But the cost of these and other benefits remains high during every period of history. The energy that first creates and then sustains civilization must be taken from the quest for perfect happiness (Nirvana), and no "higher" or "more civilized" substitute, such as the enjoyment of art or the reassurance of religion, can compensate for the loss of Nirvana.

Freud's doctrine about the conflict between pleasure and civilization amounts to the claim that the fundamental problem of reconciling (a) happiness as the aim of life with (b) survival as the precondition for happiness never can be solved to the satisfaction of both (a) and (b). This doctrine explains the inability of even affluent and highly advanced cultures to surpass the situation in which (a) and (b) remain at odds. The doctrine also offers a plausible explanation for the apparently impassable conflict between the individual and society. The individual's pursuit of absolute pleasure threatens to deprive the community of the energy it requires as both the protector of life and the provider of compensatory gratification;

hence preservation of the community demands from each of its members a sacrifice in happiness. Despite the adverse effects it has on individual happiness, however, civilization remains desirable because the species would soon perish without it. After portraying the negative in civilized life, Freud still resists the temptation to condemn civilization in favor of a new barbarism.

Freud debunks romanticism in accounts of both the individual and society. He discredits the idea that reason largely determines behavior; instead he emphasizes the extent to which behavior reflects the presence of irrational components in the self. But psychoanalysis does not side with either the instincts or their conditioned repression by the superego simply because the theory affirms the relatively minor role of reason in determining behavior. That Freudian therapy aims at securing and maintaining a position of dominance for the intellect indicates the value that Freudian theory places on rationality.

This short review of psychoanalysis has been conducted on a general level. No consideration has been given, for example, to the question of whether specific tenets in the theory translate into practice. The omission of such questions runs counter to the tradition of evaluating psychoanalysis simply on its success or failure as psychotherapy, but Freudian theory can be defended independently of Freudian therapy. To establish that psychoanalysis does not offer the best techniques for curing the mentally ill is not to prove the inadequacy of its theoretical side; the fault may lie exclusively in attempts to translate a sound theory into practice. In any case the aim here has been to present psychoanalysis as a theory of civilization that can be considered apart from the related system of psychotherapy. Of course, these two aspects of psychoanalysis cannot be separated altogether; yet the insights in the theory cannot be discounted just because Freudian therapy may have fallen into disrepute. The decision to accept or reject Freudian theory should reflect a conviction about whether the theory in comparison with its competitors affords a sufficiently broad and reliable perspective from which to view civilization and to anticipate its future course.

Ideals and Progress

The critique of utopianism has run roughly as follows. Marxism was selected as a representative of utopian social theory first because it offers a sophisticated and comprehensive account of civilization; second because its impact on history probably has been greater than that of any of its rivals. Perhaps the most telling objection against Marxism concerns its doctrine about man, which centers on the implausible thesis that man's needs do not outstrip his capacity to satisfy them. This thesis underlies Marx's vision of a society that supports both prosperity and freedom on a universal scale; hence a criticism of the thesis touched his entire theory of history. The discussion turned next to psychoanalysis as an alternative account of man and his civilization. According to Freudian theory, the need for pleasure can be fully gratified through death alone; man therefore cannot escape a fate in which the fundamental demands of his instincts remain incompatible with life itself. This somber conclusion contrasts sharply with the prediction that man can alter his lot by using a capitalist hell in order to forge a communist utopia.

Another survey of the distance that separates Marxian from Freudian theory seems unnecessary because the terrain has been mapped several times. Instead of repeating the recommendations for the Freudian alternative it might be more instructive to consider how an antiutopian theory can accommodate ideals. Ideals may contribute to progress even under the assumption that they may not become reality. Their possible contribution in this regard can be clarified by recalling the role Marx assigns to consciousness in social revolutions. A revolutionary class, such as the bourgeoisie under feudalism or the proletariat under capitalism, advances civilization if the class seizes power from the established regime; for the seizure completes a key step in the introduction of a new and presumably higher form of society. However, a suppressed class cannot be expected to risk a struggle against its rulers unless it comprehends the purpose and potential rewards of the venture;

hence Marxism, as the ideology of the proletariat, seeks to educate the class in the desirability and alleged inevitability of its revolt against the bourgeoisie.

The point now can be expressed in much more general terms as the dictum that consciousness of an ideal is a precondition for its *rational* implementation. In simpler language, social progress may occur either by accident (nonrationally) or by design (rationally), and a designed advance in civilization indicates an understanding that the future need not repeat the past and the present. Thus an ideal promotes the conviction that reality could be other than it is, and since an ideal (for instance, universal justice) furnishes a standard against which reality can be evaluated, an ideal serves as both incentive and partial guide for progress.[4] From the antiutopian perspective, however, ideals become irrational and therefore dangerous once they inspire action that cannot succeed in reaching its goal. Naturally, this perspective cannot match the appeal of a utopian vision, but antiutopianism compensates by centering on ideals within reason.

Notes

Chapter 1

1. Marx, "The German Ideology" in *Selected Works in Three Volumes* (Moscow: Progress Publishers, 1969), vol. 1, p. 47.

2. Adam Smith, *The Wealth of Nations* (New York: Random House, 1937), p. 44.

3. The phrase comes from M. Merleau-Ponty, who also talks about a dilemma of politics that arises because a revolutionary must justify present terror on the promise of its future rewards. *Humanism and Terror: An Essay on the Communist Problem* (Boston: The Beacon Press, 1969), p. xxxi.

4. Marx, *Capital: A Critical Analysis of Capitalist Production* (Moscow: Foreign Languages Publishing House, 1958), vol. 1, p. 10. For a defense of the claim that Marx's greatest contribution consists in broadening the base of natural science, see Z. A. Jordan, *The Evolution of Dialectical Materialism* (New York: St. Martin's Press, 1967), especially pp. 61ff.

5. Engels first suggested the comparison with Darwin. *Selected Writings* (Baltimore: Penguin Books, 1967), p. 204.

6. Z. A. Jordan offers such an interpretation in the work cited above.

7. Marx was surprised and dismayed when his predictions about the demise of capitalism were not fulfilled during the middle of the 19th century. For further discussion, see M. Rubel, *Karl Marx, essai de biographie intellectuelle* (Paris: Rivière, 1957).

Chapter 2

1. For Marx's own characterization of the new materialism, see "The German Ideology" in *Selected Works in Three Volumes* (Moscow: Progress Publishers, 1969), vol. 1, pp. 17-61.

2. L. Althusser, *For Marx* (London: The Penguin Press, 1969), combines ingenuity and scholarship in attempting to establish that Marx's writings fall into quite distinct periods. For an interpretation that emphasizes the continuity between Marx and the German metaphysicians, see R. Tucker, *Philosophy and Myth in Karl Marx* (Cambridge: Cambridge University Press, 1971). Finally, for a detailed statement of the position that will be adopted in this work, see I. Mészáros, *Marx's Theory of Alienation* (London: The Merlin Press, 1970).

3. Marx, "Theses on Feuerbach" in *Selected Works in Three Volumes* (Moscow: Progress Publishers, 1969), vol. 1, p. 15.

4. N. Lobkowicz offers a survey of the theory/practice distinction from Aristotle through Marx in *Theory and Practice* (South Bend, Ind: University of Notre Dame Press, 1967).

5. R. Tucker is one example; see his *Philosophy and Myth in Karl Marx* (Cambridge: Cambridge University Press, 1971).

6. The first quotation comes from R. Schacht, *Alienation* (New York: Doubleday and Company, Inc., 1971), p. 38; the others come from J. Hyppolite, "The Concept of Existence in the Hegelian Phenomenology," in *Studies on Marx and Hegel* (New York: Basic Books, 1969), p. 23.

7. Hegel, *Phänomenologie des Geistes* (Hamburg: Meiner Verlag, 1970), pp. 141-150. Sartre's analysis of masochism and sadism in sexual relationships borrows heavily from Hegel's study of mastery and slavery. *Being and Nothingness* (New York: Citadel Press, 1964), pp. 340-388.

8. Hegel does not emphasize this aspect of work, although he clearly recognizes it.

9. Hume's account of personal identity centers on the insight that consciousness cannot be equated with any one of its fleeting

contents. *A Treatise of Human Nature* (Oxford: Clarendon Press, 1964), pp. 232-262.

10. Sartre, *Being and Nothingness* (New York: Citadel Press, 1964), p. 63.

11. This explains why a Marxist interpretation of Hegel must place the category of work at the very center of Hegelianism. For an example, see A. Kojève, *Introduction to the Reading of Hegel* (New York: Basic Books, Inc., 1969).

12. Marx, "The German Ideology," in *Selected Works in Three Volumes* (Moscow: Progress Publishers, 1969), vol. 1, p. 20.

13. Marx, *Economic and Philosophic Manuscripts of 1844* (New York: International Publishers, 1969), p. 158.

14. Marx, "A Contribution to the Critique of Political Economy," in *Selected Works in One Volume* (New York: International Publishers, 1969), p. 182.

15. Marx, *Economic and Philosophic Manuscripts of 1844* (New York: International Publishers, 1969), p. 171.

16. Marx, "The German Ideology," in *Selected Works in Three Volumes* (Moscow: Progress Publishers, 1969), vol. 1, p. 17.

17. For this reason Marx talks about Feuerbach's "contemplative and inconsistent materialism." "The German Ideology" in *Selected Works in Three Volumes* (Moscow: Progress Publishers, 1969), vol. 1, pp. 27ff.

18. L. Althusser has an excellent discussion of the point in *For Marx* (London: The Penguin Press, 1969), pp. 162-218.

19. Marx, *Economic and Philosophic Manuscripts of 1844* (New York: International Publishers, 1969), pp. 109-110.

20. Marx, *Grundrisse der Kritik der politischen Ökonomie*, 2 Vols. (Berlin: Dietz Verlag, 1953), p. 716.

21. Marx, "The German Ideology" in *Selected Works in Three Volumes* (Moscow: Progress Publishers, 1969), vol. 1, p. 32.

22. For a discussion, see B. Ollman, *Alienation: Marx's Conception of Man in Capitalist Society* (Cambridge: Cambridge University Press, 1971), pp. 19ff.

23. Marx, *The Poverty of Philosophy* (New York: International Publishers, 1963), p. 131.

24. Marx, "The German Ideology," in *Selected Works in Three Volumes* (Moscow: Progress Publishers, 1969), vol. 1, p. 34.

25. Hegel, *The Phenomenology of Mind* (London: Allen and Unwin, 1964), p. 68.

Chapter 3

1. Marx's *The Poverty of Philosophy* (New York: International Publishers, 1963) is a reply to Proudhon's *The Philosophy of Poverty*. For Proudhon's statement of his own position, see *Selected Writings of P.-J. Proudhon* (New York: Doubleday and Co., 1969).

2. Marx, *Capital: A Critical Analysis of Capitalist Production* (Moscow: Foreign Languages Publishing House, 1959), vol. 3, p. 800.

3. Marx, *Historisch-kritische Gesamtausgabe* (Frankfurt: Verlagsgesellschaft, 1927), vol. 1, p. 151.

4. Marx, *Capital: A Critical Analysis of Capitalist Production* (Moscow: Foreign Languages Publishing House, 1958), vol. 1, p. 178.

5. Marx, *Economic and Philosophic Manuscripts of 1844* (New York: International Publishers, 1969), pp. 110-111.

6. Marx, *Capital: A Critical Analysis of Capitalist Production* (Moscow: Foreign Languages Publishing House, 1958), vol. 1, p. 183.

7. Marx, *Economic and Philosophic Manuscripts of 1844* (New York: International Publishers, 1969), pp. 112ff.

8. Marx, *Economic and Philosophic Manuscripts of 1844* (New York: International Publishers, 1969), p. 115.

9. Marx, "The German Ideology," in *Selected Works in Three Volumes* (Moscow: Progress Publishers, 1969), vol. 1, p. 23.

10. Marx, "The German Ideology," in *Selected Works in Three Volumes* (Moscow: Progress Publishers, 1969), vol. 1, p. 69.

11. Marx, *Economic and Philosophic Manuscripts of 1844* (New York: International Publishers, 1969), p. 107.

12. Marx, *Capital: A Critical Analysis of Capitalist Production* (Moscow: Foreign Languages Publishing House, 1958), vol. 1, p. 648.

13. For a discussion of the problem in modern America, see R. Blauner, *Alienation and Freedom: The Factory Worker and His Industry* (Chicago: University of Chicago Press, 1964).

14. Marx's expression of the point becomes most polemical in the "Manifesto of the Communist Party," in *Selected Works in One Volume* (New York: International Publishers, 1969), pp. 31-63; cf. *Ökonomische Schriften* (Stuttgart: Kröner Verlag, 1970), especially pp. 26ff.

15. Marx, *Capital: A Critical Analysis of Capitalist Production* (Moscow: Foreign Languages Publishing House, 1958), vol. 1, p. 18.

16. The so-called Paris Commune is the standard example of such a dictatorship. See Marx, "The Civil War in France" and "Critique of the Gotha Programme," in *Selected Works in One Volume* (New York: International Publishers, 1969), pp. 274-335.

17. For a summary of Marx's position in the light of modern economic theory, see K. Kühne's introduction to *Ökonomische Schriften* (Stuttgart: Kröner Verlag, 1970), pp. xviii-lxxxvii. Cf. P. A. Baran and P. M. Sweezy, *Monopoly Capital* (New York: Monthly Review Press, 1966); R. L. Meek, *Studies in the Labor Theory of Value* (New York: International Publishers, 1956); and J. Robinson, *An Essay on Marxian Economics*, 2d ed. (New York: St. Martin's Press, 1967). For a defense of Marx against his modern critics, see E. Mandel, *The Formation of the Economic Thought of Karl Marx* (New York: Monthly Review Press, 1971).

Chapter 4

1. Marx, "A Contribution to the Critique of Political Economy," in *Selected Works in One Volume* (New York: International Publishers, 1969), p. 183.

Chapter 5

1. Current examples of behaviorism are unquestionably more sophisticated than their Pavlovian ancestor; the point here, however, is that the explanatory model remains the same in the sense that *external* determinants of behavior are emphasized almost to the exclusion of internal ones.

2. For a behavioristic account of language, see B. F. Skinner, *Verbal Behavior* (New York: Appleton-Century-Crofts, 1957); for a devastating critique, see N. Chomsky, "A Review of B. F. Skinner's *Verbal Behavior*," in *The Structure of Language: Readings in the Philosophy of Language*, ed. J. A. Fodor and J. J. Katz (Englewood Cliffs, N. J.: Prentice-Hall, 1964), pp. 547-578.

Chapter 6

1. Perhaps R. D. Laing is the best known of the contemporary psychiatrists who point out the difficulty, if not the impossibility, of determining whether the individual or his society suffers from mental disorder. See, for instance, *The Divided Self* (Baltimore: Penguin Books, 1967).

2. Freud, "Anxiety and Instinctual Life," in *The Standard Edition of the Complete Psychological Works of Sigmund Freud* (London: Hogarth Press, 1964), vol. 22, p. 95.

3. Freud, "Why War?," in *The Standard Edition* (London: Hogarth Press, 1964), vol. 22, pp. 203-215.

4. Freud, *A General Introduction to Psychoanalysis* (New York: Perma Giants, 1953), p. 124.

5. Freud, "The Ego and the Id," in *The Standard Edition* (London: Hogarth Press, 1964), vol. 19, p. 34.

6. Freud himself usually talks about his "economic" conception of the self. For a discussion of the models, see P. Ricoeur, *Freud and Philosophy: An Essay in Interpretation* (New Haven, Conn.: Yale University Press, 1970).

7. For a discussion of the issue, see S. Hampshire, ed. *Philosophy of Mind* (New York: Harper and Row, 1966); and C. V. Borst, ed. *The Mind-Brain Identity Theory*)New York: St. Martin's Press, 1970).

8. This model includes but is not identical to Freud's study of the "dynamics" of the self. See "The Ego and the Id," in *The Standard Edition* (London: Hogarth Press, 1964), vol. 19, pp. 13-66.

9. Freud usually talks about the Death instincts; for the sake of convenience, however, these generally will be treated as a single drive. The material on narcissism is presented in an essay, "On Narcissism: An Introduction," in *The Standard Edition* (London: Hogarth Press, 1964), vol. 14, pp. 73-102.

10. Freud, *Beyond the Pleasure Principle* (New York: Bantam Books, 1963), pp. 67-68.

11. Freud, *Beyond the Pleasure Principle* (New York: Bantam Books, 1963), p. 98.

12. Freud, *Beyond the Pleasure Principle* (New York: Bantam Books, 1963), pp. 100-105.

13. This theme is treated at length in Chapter 7 in "The Monism of the Death Instinct."

14. Freud, *Totem und Tabu: Einige Übereinstimmungen im Seelenleben der Wilden und der Neurotiker* (Frankfurt: Fischer Verlag, 1956), especially pp. 158ff.

15. Freud's critics, notably Malinowski, have pointed out that the myth contains a serious inconsistency. It is meant to explain the *origin* of civilization through the *formation* of the superego; yet the "precivilized" brothers feel remorse only because each of them already has a superego or conscience. Thus the myth presupposes the presence of the superego in explaining its creation.

16. Freud, "Three Essays on the Theory of Sexuality," in *The Standard Edition* (London: Hogarth Press, 1960), vol. 7, p. 178.

17. Freud, *Civilization and Its Discontents* (New York: W. W. Norton and Co., 1962), p. 84.

18. Freud, *Beyond the Pleasure Principle* (New York: Bantam Books, 1959), p. 70.

Chapter 7

1. Freud's masterpiece on the analysis of dreams is *Die Traumdeutung* (Frankfurt: Fischer Verlag, 1958). Sections 6 and 7 are of special interest here. Cf. "A Metapsychological Supplement to the Theory of Dreams," in *The Standard Edition* (London: Hogarth Press, 1964), vol. 14, pp. 222-236; and "Introductory Lectures on Psychoanalysis," in *The Standard Edition* (London: Hogarth Press, 1963), vol. 15, pp. 15-448.

2. See, for instance, *Der Witz* (Frankfurt: Fischer Verlag, 1958); and *Zur Psychopathologie des Alltagslebens* (Frankfurt: Fischer Verlag, 1954).

3. Freud, *The Future of an Illusion* (New York: Doubleday and Co., 1964), pp. 87-88.

4. Freud, *The Future of an Illusion* (New York: Doubleday and Co., 1964), p. 89.

5. The essay "Analysis: Terminable and Interminable" is especially important in this regard. *The Standard Edition* (London: Hogarth Press, 1964), vol. 23, pp. 216-253.

6. Here he cites another myth, that of Empedocles, as an expression of the theory of instincts, but Freud clearly admits that such myths cannot be construed as strict evidence for his theory.

7. Marcuse comes very close to concluding that Freud's putative dualism collapses into an instinctual monism:

> If the Death instinct presses for the annihilation of life because life is the predominance of displeasure, tension, and need, then the Nirvana principle too would be a form of the pleasure principle, and the Death instinct would be dangerously close to Eros. On the other hand, Eros itself seems to partake of the nature of the Death instinct; the striving for pacification, for making pleasure eternal, indicates an instinctual resistance in Eros as well to the continual appearance of new tensions, to giving up a pleasur-

able equilibrium once reached. This resistance, if not hostile to life, is nevertheless static and thus "antagonistic to progress." Freud saw the original unity of the two opposing instincts: he spoke of the "*conservative nature*" common to them, of the "inner weight," and "inertia" of all life. He rejected this thought—in fear, one might almost say—and maintained the duality of Eros and the Death instinct, the pleasure principle and the Nirvana principle, despite the difficulty, which he emphasized several times, of demonstrating any drives in the organism other than originally libidinous ones.

"Freedom and Freud's Theory of Instincts," in *Five Lectures* (Boston: The Beacon Press, 1970), pp. 7-8; cf. "Progress and Freud's Theory of Instincts" in *Five Lectures* (Boston: The Beacon Press, 1970), pp. 28-43.

8. Marcuse, *Eros and Civilization: A Philosophical Inquiry into Freud* (New York: Vintage Books, 1962), p. 11.

9. Marcuse, *Eros and Civilization: A Philosophical Inquiry into Freud* (New York: Vintage Books, 1962), p. 97.

10. Marcuse, *One-Dimensional Man: Studies in the Ideology of Advanced Industrial Society* (Boston: The Beacon Press, 1968), p. 74.

11. For instance, *Der Witz* (Frankfurt: Fischer Verlag, 1958).

12. Marcuse, *Eros and Civilization: A Philosophical Inquiry into Freud* (New York: Vintage Books, 1962), p. 118.

13. See, for instance, L. Kolakowski, "The Psychoanalytic Theory of Culture," in *Tri-Quarterly*, vol. 22 (Fall 1972): 68-102.

14. For a Marxist defense of the terror in Russia, see M. Merleau-Ponty, *Humanism and Terror: An Essay on the Communist Problem* (Boston: The Beacon Press, 1969).

15. Freud, "The Loss of Reality in Neurosis and Psychosis," in *The Standard Edition* (London: Hogarth Press, 1964), vol. 19, p. 185.

Chapter 8

1. Kant, *Kritik der reinen Vernunft* (Würzburg: Meiner Verlag, 1956), Avii-Bxliv.

2. Verification has become one of the central problems in contemporary philosophy of science. For background, see T. Kuhn, *The Structure of Scientific Revolutions*, 2d ed. (Chicago: University of Chicago Press, 1970); and I. Lakatos and A. Musgrave, eds., *Criticism and the Growth of Knowledge* (Cambridge: Cambridge University Press, 1970). For some comments on the problem of verification in psychoanalysis, see B. F. Skinner, "Critique of Psychoanalytic Concepts and Theories," in *Minnesota Studies in the Philosophy of Science*, vol. 1 (Minneapolis: University of Minnesota Press, 1968); and P. E. Meehl, "Some Methodological Reflections on the Difficulties of Psychoanalytic Research," in *Minnesota Studies in the Philosophy of Science*, vol. 4 (Minneapolis: University of Minnesota Press, 1968), pp. 403-416.

3. For instance, see T. Kuhn, *The Copernican Revolution* (Cambridge, Mass: Harvard University Press, 1972).

4. Marcuse has an excellent essay on the topic. "The Concept of Essence," in *Negations: Essays in Critical Theory* (Boston: The Beacon Press, 1969), pp. 43-87.

Selected Bibliography

A. Marx's Works

1. German Editions
   Historisch-kritische Gesamtausgabe. Frankfurt: Marx-Engels Verlagsgesellschaft, 1927.
   Grundrisse der Kritik der Politischen Ökonomie. Berlin: Dietz Verlag, 1953.
   Werke. Berlin: Dietz Verlag, 1961.
   Ökonomische Schriften in thematischem Zusammenhang. Stuttgart: Kröner Verlag, 1970.
2. Translations
   Selected Correspondence: 1846-1895. New York: International Publishers, 1942.
   Capital: A Critical Analysis of Capitalist Production. Moscow: Foreign Languages Publishing House, 1957-59.
   The Poverty of Philosophy. New York: International Publishers, 1963.
   Writings of the Young Marx on Philosophy and Society. New York: Doubleday and Co., 1967.
   Selected Works in Three Volumes. Moscow: Progress Publishers, 1969.
   Selected Works in One Volume. New York: International Publishers, 1969.
   Economic and Philosophic Manuscripts of 1844. New York: International Publishers, 1969.
   The Eighteenth Brumaire of Louis Bonaparte. New York: International Publishers, 1969.

B. Freud's Works

1. German Editions

Gesammelte Werke. London: Imago Publishing Co., 1940.

Abriss der Psychoanalyse. Frankfurt: Fischer Verlag, 1953.

Das Unbehagen in der Kultur. Frankfurt: Fischer Verlag, 1953.

Zur Psychopathologie des Alltagslebens. Frankfurt: Fischer Verlag, 1954.

Totem und Tabu: Einige Übereinstimmungen im Seelenleben der Wilden und der Neurotiker. Frankfurt: Fischer Verlag, 1956.

Der Witz und Seine Beziehung zum Unbewussten. Frankfurt: Fischer Verlag, 1959.

Die Traumdeutung. Frankfurt: Fischer Verlag, 1961.

Drei Abhandlungen zur Sexualtheorie. Frankfurt: Fischer Verlag, 1961.

2. Translations

Collected Papers. London: International Psychoanalytic Press, 1924.

The Standard Edition of the Complete Psychological Works of Sigmund Freud. London: Hogarth Press, 1953-64.

A General Introduction to Psychoanalysis. New York: Perma Giants, 1953.

The Origin and Development of Psychoanalysis. Chicago: Henry Regnery Co., 1953.

Civilization and Its Discontents. New York: W. W. Norton Co., 1962.

Beyond the Pleasure Principle. New York: Bantam Books, 1963.

The Future of an Illusion. New York: Doubleday and Co., 1964.

C. Other Works

Adler, M. *Lehrbuch der materialistischen Geschichtsauffassung.* Berlin: Laub Verlag, 1930.

Adorno, T. *Aspekte der Hegelschen Philosophie.* Frankfurt: Suhrkamp Verlag, 1957.

Althusser, L. *For Marx.* London: The Penguin Press, 1969.

——. *Lenin and Philosophy and Other Essays.* New York: Monthly Review Press, 1971.

Axelos, K. *Marx, penseur de la technique.* Paris: Editions de Minuit, 1961.

Bakunin, M. *The Political Philosophy of Bakunin.* New York: The Free Press, 1964.

Baran, P., and Sweezy, P. *Monopoly Capital.* New York: Monthly Review Press, 1966.

Benner, D. *Theorie und Praxis.* Wien: Oldenbourg Verlag, 1966.

Bernstein, E. *Die Arbeiterbewegung.* Frankfurt: Rütten und Leonig, 1910.

Blauner, R. *Alienation and Freedom: The Factory Worker and His Industry.* Chicago: University of Chicago Press, 1964.

Bloch, E. *On Karl Marx.* New York: Herder and Herder, 1971.

Brown, N. O. *Life against Death: The Psychoanalytic Meaning of History.* Middletown, Conn.: Wesleyan University Press, 1959.

——. *Love's Body.* New York: Vintage Books, 1966.

Calvez, J.-Y. *La pensée de Karl Marx.* Paris: Editions du Seuil, 1956.

Cornu, A. *Karl Marx et la révolution de 1848.* Paris: Presses Universitaires de France, 1948.

Dahrendorf, R. *Class and Class Conflict in Industrial Society.* Stanford, Calif.: Stanford University Press, 1970.

Dalbiez, R. *Psychoanalytical Method and the Doctrine of Freud.* London: Longmans, Green and Co., 1948.

Engels, F. *Selected Writings.* Baltimore: Penguin Books, 1967.

Ferenczi, S. *Sex in Psychoanalysis.* New York: Basic Books, 1950.

——. *Further Contributions to the Theory and Technique of Psychoanalysis.* New York: Basic Books, 1952.

————. *Final Contributions to the Problems and Methods of Psychoanalysis*. London: Hogarth Press, 1955.

Feuer, L. *Marx and the Intellectuals*. New York: Doubleday and Co., 1969.

Friedrich, M. *Philosophie und Ökonomie beim jungen Marx*. Berlin: Dietz Verlag, 1960.

Fromm, E. *Beyond the Chains of Illusion*. New York: Simon and Schuster, 1962.

————. *Socialist Humanism*. New York: Doubleday and Co., 1966.

Gay, P. *The Dilemma of Democratic Socialism*. New York: Collier Books, 1970.

Habermas, J. *Theorie und Praxis*. Neuwied: Luchterhand Verlag, 1963.

Hegel, G. *Phänomenologie des Geistes*. Hamburg: Meiner Verlag, 1952.

————. *The Phenomenology of Mind*. London: Allen and Unwin, 1964.

Heiss, R. *Die grossen Dialektiker des 19. Jahrhunderts*. Köln and Berlin: Kiepenheuer and Witsch, 1963.

Hook, S. *From Hegel to Marx: Studies in the Intellectual Development of Karl Marx*. 2d ed. Ann Arbor: University of Michigan Press, 1962.

Horney, K. *New Ways in Psychoanalysis*. New York: W. W. Norton Co., 1939.

Hyppolite, J. *Genèse et structure de la Phénoménologie de l'Esprit de Hegel*. Paris: Aubier, 1946.

————. *Studies on Marx and Hegel*. New York: Basic Books, 1969.

Jones, E. *Sigmund Freud: Life and Work*. New York: Basic Books, 1953.

Jordan, Z. A. *The Evolution of Dialectical Materialism*. New York: St. Martin's Press, 1967.

Kamenka, E. *The Ethical Foundations of Marxism*. New York: Praeger, 1962.

Kant, I. *Kritik der reinen Vernunft.* Würzburg: Meiner Verlag, 1956.

Kautsky, K. *Die materialistische Geschichtsauffassung.* Berlin: Dietz Verlag, 1927.

Kolakowski, L. *Toward a Marxist Humanism.* New York: Grove Press, 1969.

————. "A Leszek Kolakowski Reader." *Tri-Quarterly*, vol. 22 (Fall 1971).

Kojève, A. *Introduction to the Reading of Hegel.* New York: Basic Books, 1969.

Korsch, K. *Karl Marx.* New York: Russell and Russell, 1963.

————. *Die materialistische Geschichtsauffassung.* Leipzig: Lichtenstein, 1929.

Lefèbvre, H. *The Sociology of Marx.* New York: Vintage Books, 1969.

Lenin, V. *Collected Works.* Moscow: Progress Publishers, n.d.

Lichteim, G. *Marxism: An Historical and Critical Study.* New York: Praeger Publishers, 1970.

Lobkowicz, N. *Theory and Practice: History of a Concept from Aristotle to Marx.* South Bend, Ind.: University of Notre Dame Press, 1967.

Löwith, K. *Von Hegel zu Nietzsche.* Stuttgart: Kohlhammer Verlag, 1958.

Lukács, G. *Geschichte und Klassenbewusstsein.* Berlin: Malik Verlag, 1923.

————. *Der junge Hegel: Über die Beziehung von Dialetik und Ökonomie.* Zürich-Wien: Europa Verlag, 1948.

————. *Die Zerstörung der Vernunft.* Neuwied: Luchterhand, 1962.

Mandel E. *The Formation of the Economic Thought of Karl Marx.* New York: Monthly Review Press, 1971.

Marcuse, H. *Reason and Revolution: Hegel and the Rise of Social Theory.* Boston: The Beacon Press, 1960.

————. *Soviet Marxism: A Critical Analysis.* New York: Vintage Books, 1961.

————. *Eros and Civilization: A Philosophical Inquiry into Freud.* New York: Vintage Books, 1962.

————. *One-Dimensional Man: Studies in the Ideology of Advanced Industrial Society.* Boston: The Beacon Press, 1968.

————. *An Essay on Liberation.* Boston: The Beacon Press. 1969.

————. *Negations: Essays in Critical Theory.* Boston: The Beacon Press, 1969.

————. *Five Lectures.* Boston: The Beacon Press, 1970.

————. *Counterrevolution and Revolt.* Boston: The Beacon Press, 1972.

Meek, R. *Studies in the Labor Theory of Value.* New York: International Publishers, 1956.

Merleau-Ponty, M. *Humanism and Terror: An Essay on the Communist Problem.* Boston: The Beacon Press, 1969.

Mészáros, I. *Marx's Theory of Alienation.* London: Merlin Press, 1970.

Mills, C. W. *The Marxists.* New York: Dell Publishing Co., 1962.

Ollman, B. *Alienation: Marx's Conception of Man in Capitalist Society.* Cambridge: Cambridge University Press, 1971.

Popitz, H. *Der entfremdete Mensch: Zeitkritik und Geschichts-philosophie des jungen Marx.* Basel: Verlag für Recht und Gesellschaft, 1953.

Proudhon, P.-J. *Selected Writings.* New York: Doubleday and Co., 1969.

Ricoeur, P. *Freud and Philosophy: An Essay on Interpretation. New Haven, Conn.: Yale University Press, 1970.*

Rieff, P. *Freud: The Mind of the Moralist.* New York: Anchor Books, 1961.

Robinson, J. *An Essay on Marxian Economics.* New York: St. Martin's Press, 1967.

Robinson, P. *The Freudian Left.* New York: Colophon Books, 1969.

Roszak, T. *The Making of a Counter Culture*. New York: Anchor Books, 1969.

Rotenstreich, N. *Basic Problems of Marx's Philosophy*. New York: Bobbs-Merrill Co., 1965.

Rubel, M. *Karl Marx, essai d'une biographie intellectuelle*. Paris: Rivière, 1957.

Schacht, R. *Alienation*. New York: Doubleday and Co., 1971.

Schaff, A. *Marxism and the Human Individual*. New York: McGraw-Hill Co., 1970.

Schmidt, A. *The Concept of Nature in Marx*. London: NLB Publishers, 1971.

Sebag, L. *Marxismus und Strukturalismus*. Frankfurt: Suhrkamp Verlag, 1967.

Tönnies, F. *Marx: Leben und Lehre*. Jena: Lichtenstein, 1921.

Trilling, L. *Freud and the Crisis of Our Culture*. Boston: The Beacon Press, 1955.

Tucker, R. *Philosophy and Myth in Karl Marx*. Cambridge: Cambridge University Press, 1961.

————. *The Marxian Revolutionary Idea*. New York: W. W. Norton Co., 1970.

Index

absolute spirit, 20-1, 23, 27-30, 32, 47

action (activity). *See* practice

aggression, 124, 140, 145, 166, 180, 189

agriculture, 26, 66, 103, 139, 145, 178

alienation (estrangement), 4, 15, 42, 54, 64, 85, 87, 89, 91, 93, 98, 104-5, 111
and division of labor, 68-70, 74
from fellow men, 61-3, 83
from generic potentialities, 61-3, 78
and private property, 72-4
from product, 55-8, 60, 62-3, 83
from productive activity, 58-60, 62-3, 78

Althusser, L., 202-3

ambivalence, 156, 176, 189, 197

analogy, 87, 125, 138

Ananke, trans. of, 150
as Reality, 153, 169

antagonism, 25, 52-3, 57, 63, 65, 89, 121, 123, 150, 155, 161, 176, 196, 209

antiutopianism, x, xi, 112, 117, 194, 199, 200

anxiety, 26, 174, 179-81, 189

appropriation, 26, 57-9. *See also* labor; work

aristocracy, 39, 66-7, 92

Aristophanes, 152

Aristotle, 38, 202

art, 16, 123, 133, 158, 173, 187-9, 197

artisan, 26, 66, 69

assembly line, 56, 59, 75

authority, 66, 128-30, 135, 137, 139-40, 156, 181

autoeroticism, 142-3

automation, 78, 95, 105
and alienation, 93-4

avarice. *See* greed

Baran, P., 205n

behaviorism, 113-6, 206n

biogenetic law, 118-9, 134, 137, 154

About the Author

Martin G. Kalin, Ph.D.

Since 1969, Dr. Kalin has been assistant professor of philosophy at DePaul University in Chicago.

He received his B.S. degree from Loyola University (Chicago), and his M.A. and Ph.D. degrees in philosophy from Northwestern University.

As a Fulbright-Hays Fellow, he studied at the Heidelberg University in West Germany. Also, he did further study under a Carnegie Foundation Grant for the Institute in the Philosophy of Language at the University of California at Irvine.

Dr. Kalin's articles on philosophical subjects have appeared in professional magazines. His papers have been presented at the national convention of the American Psychology Association and at several leading universities. He lives with his wife in Chicago.